THEME WA
GLOUCESTE

Gordon Ottewell

Thornhill Press
24 Moorend Road
Cheltenham, Glos.

MCMLXXXIX

© Gordon Ottewell

ISBN 0946328 25 0

Printed by
Devonshire Press Ltd, Torquay

Cover Design: Geoffrey Maynard

ABOUT THE AUTHOR

A native of Derbyshire, Gordon Ottewell has lived in Gloucestershire for almost 20 years. For the past ten years, his 'In the Country' column has appeared in the 'Gloucestershire Echo' and he broadcasts on BBC Radio Gloucestershire.

His books include:

'Wildlife Walks in the North Cotswolds' (Thornhill Press).
'A Cotswold Quiz Book' (Barn Owl Books).
'Gloucestershire — A Country Quiz Book' (Barn Owl Books).
'A Hereford and Worcester Quiz Book (Barn Owl Books).
'Warde Fowler's Countryside' (Severn House).
'Family Walks in the Cotswolds' (Scarthin Books).
'Family Walks in Hereford and Worcester' (Scarthin Books).

CONTENTS

PHOTOGRAPHS

ACKNOWLEDGEMENTS

I am indebted to three people in particular for help with this book.

Stan Betterton, who has known and loved the Forest well for many years, gave freely of his time, knowledge and infectious enthusiasm. Mary Hopkins read the proofs and made many invaluable suggestions. Margaret, my wife, encouraged and supported me throughout and was responsible for the typing.

I acknowledge my debt also to those fellow walkers who have helped to keep the paths open and those authors whose writings have helped me to discover the Gloucestershire landscape.

My grateful thanks to all.

Gordon Ottewell

Locations of Walks

INTRODUCTION

Gloucestershire is a superb walking county. Consisting as it does of a unique mix of forest, vale and wold, it offers the walker a range of scenic variety that few other counties can match.

It is hardly surprising, therefore, that Gloucestershire has given rise to a vast number of walks books. Many of these concentrate exclusively on the Cotswolds, while still more confine themselves to route descriptions, with the odd paragraph on things of interest to be seen on the way thrown in for good measure.

By contrast, this book ranges over the entire county and offers a distinct theme for each of the 25 walks described. Informative text relating to the theme is given in a separate section – not only to avoid confusion in the field but also to enable those wishing to use the book solely as a concise route-guide to do so.

It goes without saying that the brief section on the theme is nothing more than an introduction to the subject. Walkers wishing to extend their knowledge are referred to the 'Recommended reading' heading in the preliminary notes provided with each walk. Incidentally, many of the books mentioned in this far-from exhaustive section are out of print but they can often be borrowed from a library or obtained from second-hand bookshops.

Another point perhaps worth mentioning is that the chosen themes need not restrict the scope of the walks. One of the joys of country walking is that things of interest have a habit of cropping up in unexpected places. For instance, I am often sidetracked on one of my favourite local woodland walks by the presence nearby of the site of an abandoned medieval village. Nature-lovers will, of course, know that every walk is a nature walk, as I was reminded constantly when researching this book.

Advice may be useful about what to wear. Whatever the season or weather conditions, *strong shoes are absolutely essential.* Many of the paths can be extremely muddy after rain and there is nothing worse than tramping for miles in wet feet! Comfortable clothing, too, is vital. This means a combination of warmth, lightness and weather resistance – a matter for personal preference of course, but remember that inappropriate attire can ruin a walk.

Finally, a word about how the walks are arranged. This is largely on a regional basis, starting with the Vale of Severn, followed by the Forest of Dean and ending with the Cotswolds, working roughly northwards. The length of the walks varies from about 5 to 12 miles. The order does not necessarily mean that the easiest walks come near the front of the book – please refer to the 'Summary of terrain' note at the start of each description.

Gordon Ottewell,
June 1989

THE SKETCH MAPS

The sketch maps accompanying the walks are drawn to a scale of 1¼ inches to 1 mile (1:50 000), apart from the following exceptions: Walks 3, 6 and 8 — drawn to a scale of 2½ inches to 1 mile, and Walk 16 — drawn to a scale of 1¾ inches to 1 mile.

Map symbols
The following symbols are used on the maps:

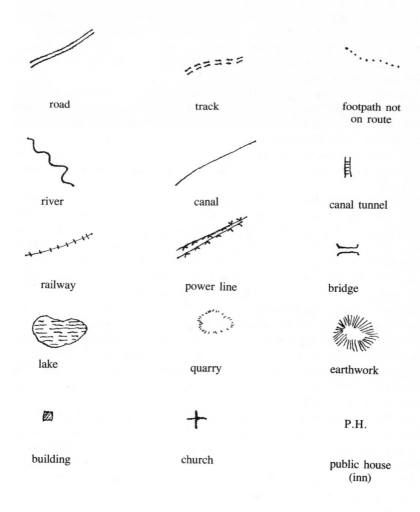

road	track	footpath not on route
river	canal	canal tunnel
railway	power line	bridge
lake	quarry	earthwork
building	church	P.H. public house (inn)

Old Passage Inn, Arlingham

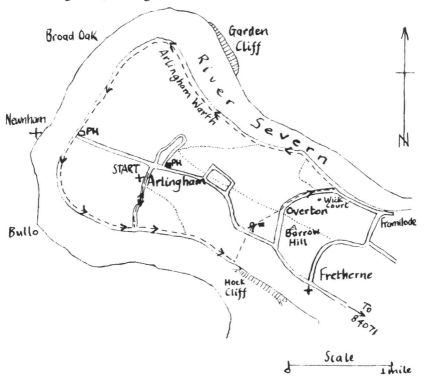

Walk 1

Around Arlingham — a Severn Estuary walk.

Theme: The Severn estuary, as seen from the loop in the river near the village of Arlingham.

Start and finish: Arlingham village.

Getting there: Arlingham lies 3 miles NW of the B4071 at Frampton-on-Severn and 5 miles west of the A38.

Route of walk: Arlingham village — Hock Cliff — Overton — Arlingham Warth — The Passage Inn — Arlingham village.

Distance: 9 miles.

Summary of terrain: Flat throughout. Flooding possible during winter and at time of Severn bores.

O.S. Sheet: Landranger 162 — Gloucester & Forest of Dean (1¼ inches to 1 mile).

Starting point grid ref: 708109.

Parking: Arlingham village.

Refreshments: The Passage Inn, Arlingham. The Red Lion Inn, Arlingham.

Recommended reading: Severn Tide, Brian Waters, Dent, 1947 (reprinted: Alan Sutton, 1987). The Severn Bore, Fred Rowbotham, David & Charles, 1964.

Theme

Although brief glimpses of the River Severn can be had on other walks in this collection, this is the only walk routed almost entirely along the river bank. This is made possible because the Severn forms a gigantic loop near the village of Arlingham, travelling nine miles to progress little more than one, and the public footpath around this loop provides a unique opportunity to take a close look at the estuary and at the riverside features that make it so distinctive.

Arlingham itself has little affinity with the river. Situated in the centre of the loop, it has no boats and its inhabitants have always obtained their livelihoods from the land rather than from the water. Dairy farming accounts for much of the land but a few of the cider and perry orchards for which the place was once famed still survive. Even so, the close proximity of a river notorious for its treachery — flooding and the effects of the Severn bore — has always influenced the people's lives. Flooding is nowadays kept under control, as can be seen on the walk, but between 1483 and 1703, no less than five disastrous floods brought much loss of life and destruction of property to Arlingham — a heavy price to pay for its otherwise enviable situation.

Arlingham owes its place in history to its ancient river-crossing to

Newnham on the Severn's west bank. There is a tradition — reinforced by the discovery some years ago of huge bones in the river near Newnham — that the Romans used elephants to effect their crossing at low tide to suppress the Britons of the Forest of Dean. Certainly we know that a passage existed over the sands, centuries later and that it was used by drovers and travellers wishing to avoid Gloucester and by a farmer to convey his livestock over to his new farm at Arlingham from Littledean before the river altered its course in 1802.

The Passage Inn reminds us of the importance of this crossing, which had its own ferry until comparatively recent times. The sea wall was begun in the 14th century when Lord Berkeley, the local landowner, decided to employ his private army in the task of repelling the sea during a lull in the Hundred Years' War.

The walk passes close to Hock Cliff, the lower Lias clays and banks of limestone of which are rich in fossils, including Devil's toenails, belemnites, sea lilies and ammonites. Another fossil-rich cliff, Garden Cliff, near Westbury-on-Severn, can be seen across the estuary on the last stage of the walk.

Hock Cliff is notable also for its association with the Severn Bore. Formed a short distance downstream where the water is held back in the narrow part of the river at Sharpness, this tidal phenomenon is caused when the rate of flow is accelerated and the water rushes on to meet the 'steps' of hard limestone rock on the river bed, followed by a wide, shallow stretch of sand near Frampton. It is said that the sound of the bore crashing on the rocks at the foot of Hock Cliff can be heard a mile away on a still night.

Walkers equipped with binoculars can be certain of enjoying both the distant views and the bird life during the course of this walk. The fine spire of Westbury church and the elegant old town of Newnham are the most prominent features visible. Bird watchers are sure to see herons feeding by the streams and standing motionless in the shallows. Cormorants fly regularly low along the river and a variety of gulls, geese, ducks and waders can be observed, depending on the season.

Route directions

Walk along the road indicated by a 'No through road' symbol, opposite the Red Lion Inn. Pass the church. Ignore a footpath sign at a sharp right-hand bend. Soon the road becomes a track, which ends at a stile. Cross and climb the bank to the river.

Turn left over stiles. Yellow arrows and dots indicate the way. Leave the river just before reaching Hock Cliff (which can be approached over a stile).

Cross marked stiles, eventually passing between hedges to reach a road at Overton. Cross, and go along a lane, leaving over a stile on the left between houses. Keeping a hedge on the right, climb to a stile at a road. (Those wishing to climb Barrow Hill should follow the footpath signposted 'Fretherne and Saul', straight ahead).

Turn left along the road. After passing the drive to Wick Court on the right, turn left over a stile signposted 'Severn Way Path' where the road bends sharply to the right at a house.

This stretch of the riverside path can be very muddy after rain or following the passing of a bore. Soon however, the path climbs to a higher level through bushes. Eventually, beyond a power line, the route follows a raised bank by the river over Arlingham Warth.

Ignore a path to Arlingham by a drain. Instead, keep straight on along the riverside path to reach the Passage Inn.

From the inn, continue along the riverside path as far as the point where the river walk commenced, indicated in the distance by two pylons.

Cross the stile and return along the lane walked earlier back to Arlingham.

Manor Farm, Frampton

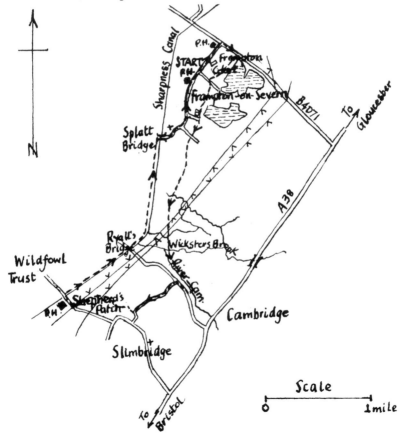

Walk 2

Nature around the village — the flora — and fauna — of Frampton.

Theme: Frampton-on-Severn — the village that gave rise to 'The Frampton Flora', the book of wild-flower paintings produced by members of the Clifford family during the early 19th century.

Start and finish: Car park by post office on village green, Frampton.

Getting there: Frampton-on-Severn lies on the B4071, 1½ miles west of the A38.

Route of walk: Frampton-on-Severn (village green) — Shepherd's Patch — Gloucester and Sharpness Canal — Splatt Bridge — Church End — Frampton village green.

Distance: 7½ miles.

Summary of terrain: Flat throughout. Footpaths muddy in winter.

O.S. Sheet: Landranger 162 — Gloucester and Forest of Dean (1¼ inches to 1 mile).

Starting point: grid ref: 749081.

Parking: Car park by post office, village green.

Refreshments: Tudor Arms, Shepherd's Patch. Bell Inn and Three Horseshoes, Frampton.

Recommended reading: The Frampton Flora, Richard Mabey (Editor), Century, 1985.

Recommended to visit: Severn Wildfowl Trust, Slimbridge.

Theme

Between 1828 and 1851, eight ladies, members of the Clifford family of Frampton Court, compiled a collection of over 200 watercolour paintings of the wild flowers of the district around Frampton-on-Severn. For 130 years the collection, mounted in three small leather-bound books, lay forgotton in an attic at Frampton Court, but in 1985 the paintings, together with an informative text by Richard Mabey, were published in book form under the title 'The Frampton Flora'. Understandably enough, the book aroused a great deal of interest both in Gloucestershire and further afield, not only on account of the excellence of the paintings, but also because of the light thrown on the lives of so-called 'ladies of leisure' in the early years of the Victorian era.

The 'Flora' apart, Frampton and its surrounding area makes an ideal subject for a natural history theme walk. The 22-acre village green — one of the largest in England — offers an unusually rich habitat for wildlife. Grassland, ponds, wet margins and mature trees all ensure that flowers, insects and birds are well provided for. Further diversity is offered by the lakes formed by gravel extraction nearby – these attract large numbers of wildfowl, some of which, including mallard and teal (dabbling ducks), tufted duck (diving duck), coot, great-crested and little grebe and Canada goose – breed on the pools. Other wildfowl, such as wigeon, pochard, pintail and shoveler, augment the winter bird population, as also do cormorants, herons and wagtails, while several species of wading birds are recorded during migration.

Despite its name, Frampton is not actually on the bank of the Severn. Instead, it is the Gloucester and Sharpness Canal, completed in 1827, that borders the village on the west and, while not in itself especially rich in wildlife, provides botanical interest along its towpath and gives good views of the drainage ditches and reed beds along the estuary.

The concluding stages of the walk, through the village from Church End, reveal why Frampton rates so highly among Gloucestershire's most attractive villages. St. Mary's church, with its Clifford monuments, old, well-maintained buildings of mellow red-brick, weathered stone and timber-framing, with roofs of pantiles and thatch – all grouped elegantly round Rosamund's Green – provide interest all the way. The name Rosamund refers to Jane Clifford, daughter of Walter, lord of the manor in the 12th century. She is said to have been born at the old manor house – now Manor Farm – and her beauty to have so captivated King Henry II that he made her his mistress, under the name Fair Rosamund.

But it is the steps of later Clifford ladies that this walk follows – by village green, over meadows, along hedgerows, by dyke and river. For these country women were happy to paint – for their own delight and now ours to share – the common flowers of the Gloucestershire countryside. And we too, as we walk around Frampton can enjoy the same flowers – lady's smock, dove-foot cranesbill, bird's foot trefoil, self heal, speedwell, ground ivy, and many more. While for those who take the trouble to study the Frampton Flora, there is an extra satisfaction, in the words of Richard Mabey: "We can look across the hundred-and-fifty years (it is only five generations after all) that separate us from the Clifford women, and see more clearly not only what has changed in our countryside but to what degree our responses to it have remained the same.'

Route Directions

Walk along the B4071 for a short distance towards the A38 (no pavement). Go through a handgate just beyond ornamental gates on the right. The footpath keeps a lake on the left. Frampton Court can be seen on the right. Eventually the path crosses a field diagonally to a stile by a cottage. Cross a lane and another stile opposite and keep a fence on the right to the next stile.

Now cross a field, aiming for a barn. Go over 3 more stiles by the barn and keep a fence on the left as far as another stile. The path now passes between two lakes, crosses the end of a road, and passes between hedges. Ignore side paths and follow the path signposted to Cambridge and Slimbridge through 3 gates. Veer diagonally across a field to another gate. In the next field, keep a hedge on the right. Slimbridge church spire can be seen slightly to the left ahead.

Cross a stile and keep a hedge on the left in the next field. Go through another gate and over a dyke. Cross the next field to a stile near the right-hand corner. Pass under power lines, heading for the tip of the spire ahead. Cross a stile by a gate, go through another gate and keep a hedge on the left. Climb the bank and cross a footbridge over Wicksters Brook to reach the River Cam over a field.

Turn left along the river bank for about ½ mile and cross a bridge and a stile to reach a road. Turn right along it and then left along Longaston Lane. When the lane bends to the left at a bungalow, cross a stile on the right and follow yellow arrows over two fields, then a farm track, a plank bridge and a stile. Over the next two fields keep the hedge on the right. At the next stile, follow the left-hand arrow and the ditch and hedge on the left. Go through 4 gates to reach a road. Turn right. The Tudor Arms is opposite.

To continue the walk, keep on over the canal bridge. (The Wildfowl Trust is straight on). Follow the towpath on the right, passing the bridge near Ryalls Farm and returning to Frampton over Splatts Bridge. The car park in at the far end of the green.

King Charles II Oak, Churchill Inclosure,
Forest of Dean

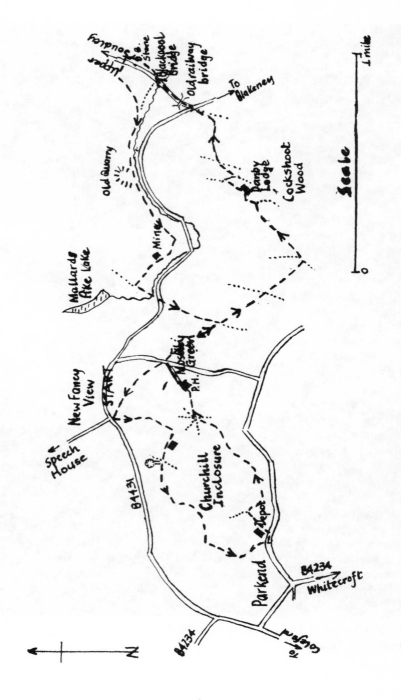

N

Scale

0   1 mile

Sounds
Sudbrook
Stone
Blackpool bridge
Old railway bridge
To Blakeney
Old Quarry
Danby Lodge
Cockshoot Wood
Mine
Mallards Pike Lake
Mostly Green
P.H.
New Fancy View
Speech House
START
B4431
Churchill Inclosure
Depot
Parkend
B4234
Whitecroft
B4234
To Coleford

16

Walk 3

Gloucestershire's Forest — Deep in the Dean

Theme: Forestry — its history and practice — as seen in a typical area of Dean.

Start and finish: Car park opposite T-junction formed by B4431 (Blakeney-Coleford road) and minor road connecting with B4226 near Speech House.

Getting there: The forest car park lies alongside the B4431, 5 miles southeast of Coleford and 4 miles northwest of Blakeney.

Route of walk: Car park — Churchill Inclosure — Parkend — Moseley Green — Danby Lodge — Blackpool Bridge — Drummer Boy Stone — Mallards Pike Lake — Moseley Green — car park.

Distance: 7 miles.

Summary of terrain: Undulating throughout. A few steady climbs but nothing formidable.

O.S. Sheet: Landranger 162 — Gloucester and Forest of Dean. (1¼ inches to 1 mile).

Starting point grid ref: 629092.

Parking: Forest car park (see above).

Refreshments: Rising Sun Inn, Moseley Green.

Recommended reading: Forest of Dean, F.W. Baty, Hale 1952.
Dean Forest and Wye Valley (Forest Park Guide), HMSO, 1964.
Current Forestry Commission leaflets.

Theme

The Forest of Dean is one of the most important remnants of the great Royal Forests of England. Its history makes fascinating reading, and is littered with such famous names as Sir Francis Drake, Sir Walter Raleigh, the diarists Pepys and Evelyn and Admiral Lord Nelson — all of whom were concerned at some stage with the production of timber for shipbuilding as part of the vital matter of national defence.

Yet despite the involvement of such notable men, the history of Dean is largely one of wasteful exploitation. Some re-planting was carried out during Stuart times (as can be seen in Churchill Inclosure) but it was not until the appointment of Edward Machen as Deputy Surveyor early in the 19th century that a concerted attempt was made to restore the Forest to something approaching its former state. Between 1810 and 1816, Machen supervised the planting of the 11,000 acres of designated as the extent of the Forest, using a mixture of oak, Spanish chestnut, larch, fir, beech and sycamore. Despite the depredations caused by vermin, disease and severe weather, and the fact that until the 1850s, many of the oaks were felled to provide timber for wooden warships, Machen's re-stocking policy, backed up by establishing of 50 acres of tree-nurseries, finally paid off. Adjustments in policy early in the present century resulted in an intensification of conifer-planting, and with the creation of the Forestry Commission in 1924, this practice was extended.

In 1938, Dean became the first area in England to be declared a Forest Park. Now extending over some 22,000 acres, it is unique in that it performs the dual function of providing timber while at the same time allowing widespread public access. This means that visitors can ramble at will through much of this vast wooded area, making use of the network of rides and other paths. The opportunity exists to see routine forestry operations — planting, weeding, thinning and felling — as well as such necessary tasks as maintaining roads, drains and fences.

No glimpse of the Forest, however brief, would be complete without a look at the trees themselves. The first stage of the walk, through Churchill Inclosure, provides an ideal opportunity to see trees of many species planted over several centuries. These range from the few surviving late 17th century oaks, including the Charles II Oak, and the oaks planted by Machen early in the last century, seen at the beginning of the walk — to the nursery of young trees opposite the entrance to the Forestry Commission depot at Parkend.

Of the hardwood trees, beech comes second only to oak and can be seen as a later planting alongside the oak in Churchill Inclosure, providing an eventual succession. Conifers, intended for an early economic return, include Douglas Fir, American Silver Fir, Corsican Pine, Norway Spruce and the deciduous European Larch. These plantings are thinned periodically, as can be seen from gaps left between the rows of trees. Notices such as 'Oak grafting' and 'Oak thinning' give some idea of the processes that have resulted in the present appearance of the woodland.

Worth noting especially are the wellingtonias seen on the right after the red-topped post. This tree is usually found as a single specimen in parks but here several can be studied not only in their mature state but also after coppicing. Beyond the wellingtonias, on the left down a slope, can be seen some fine wild cherries, while along the stream below, an avenue of hybrid poplars thrive in the damp conditions.

Route Directions

Go along the forest road into Churchill Inclosure. Keep right at a fork and right again to pass a 'Private Access' sign at Churchill Lodge. Cross a metalled road, passing the Charles II Oak on the right and take the track between the pines. At a fork, keep straight on past a red-topped fence post. At a cross track, turn left and then right in 40 yards at a fork. There follows a gradual descent to a T-junction of paths. Turn left here and keep straight on by overgrown colliery waste to reach a road. Parkend is downhill on the right.

The route now turns uphill (notice tree-nursery across the road) before going left into the Forestry Commission depot (site of the old Castlemain Colliery). Bear right and enter woodland over a stile on the right near gates. Follow the climbing track between red markers, ignoring side tracks. Cross another stile by a gate to reach a meeting of paths. Take the right-hand path, passing an 'Oak fellings' notice, with a power line overhead, and drop down to the Rising Sun Inn.

From the inn, descend the drive to cross a road and dismantled railway line and enter a coniferous wood. Go over a cross track and climb beneath a power line, keeping straight on to the top of the rise. Here, by pole No. XSA 72 (yellow marker, 15 feet up), turn left at right angles to follow a fence on the right, bordering a field. Keep on this line as far as a clearing with an old adit mine on the left. Turn left, passing the gate to Danby Lodge on the right and then follow red arrows to the right along the Lodge wall. At a T-junction, turn right and soon sharply left down a steep wooded slope. Cross a wide forest track, continuing the descent along a grassy track opposite. Keep a fence on the right as far as a conifer clump, beyond which is a T-junction of paths. Turn left here and descend to the B4431.

Cross the road and go under Blackpool Bridge. The well-known section of old road can be seen on the left. Cross a bridge and keep on along the road. When a track meets the road on the right, turn off the road to follow the right bank of the stream for about 200 yards to the Drummer Boy Stone (an artificial hollow containing smelted iron of uncertain date). Cross the stream and the road and climb by the red barrier into the woods. At a cross path, turn left over a stile and keep straight on along the narrow path to meet a track coming in from the left below. Keep on along this track, roughly parallel to the road below on the left. After passing a large abandoned quarry on the right, the route climbs, first by Douglas firs, then by beeches, before passing an adit mine on the right and descending towards Mallards Pike lake (visible through the trees) and left to reach the B4431 once more.

Cross and climb the forest track as far as the power line walked along earlier. Turn right here to retrace steps to the road below the Rising Sun. Instead of climbing the drive, take the grassy track alongside into the woods. Go over a cross track and keep straight on through the wood back to the start.

Darkhill Furnace, near Parkend

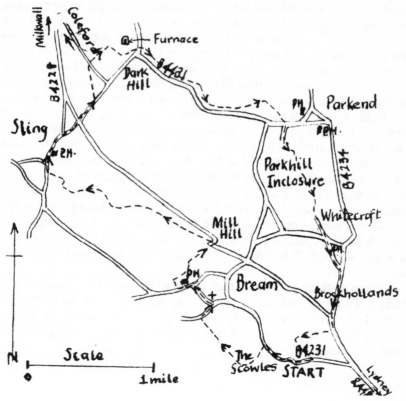

Walk 4

Forest coal and iron – Bream and beyond

Theme: The industrial archaeology of the southern area of the Forest of Dean.

Start and finish: Choice of two laybys, on either side of the B4231, approximately a mile south of Bream.

Getting there: The laybys off the B4231 south of Bream are 2miles NW of the A48 at Lydney.

Route of walk: B4231 – Bream Scowles – Bream – Mill Hill – Noxon Park – Orepool Inn – Sling – Darkhill – Parkend – Parkhill Inclosure – Whitecroft – Brockhollands – B4231 layby.

Distance: 9 miles.

Summary of terrain: Generally easy going on roads and well-surfaced tracks.

O.S. Sheet: Landranger 162 – Gloucester & Forest of Dean (1¼ inches to 1 mile).

Starting point grid ref.: 610047.

Parking: Layby (see above).

Refreshments: Orepool Inn, Sling. Woodman and Fountain inns, Parkend. Royal Oak, Whitecroft.

Recommended reading: The Old Industries of Dean, David E. Bick, 1980. Industrial Archaeology in Gloucestershire. Glos. Soc for Ind. Arch., 1975. Forest Miner, A. Marfell, Forest Bookshop, Coleford, 1980.

Recommended visits: The Dean Heritage Centre, Soudley. Clearwell Caves (ancient iron mines).

Theme

It is difficult for the modern visitor to realise that the Forest of Dean was, until quite recently, a highly industrialised area. In 1880, for instance, its 60 collieries produced a total output of over 750,000 tons of coal and its 36 iron mines yielded 90,000 tons of ore.

These mineral deposits gave rise to several processing industries, including smelting, steel making, tinplate manufacturing and wiremaking – all of which, together with mining, provided employment for most of the male population. Now, all have disappeared apart from a little coal mining carried out in the traditional way by 'free' miners.

Despite the widespread sweeping-away of this aspect of the Dean's past, there is much to interest the industrial archaeologist – and the curious walker. In terms of age, the mining of iron ore pre-dates all other evidence of industrial activity in the Forest, and the so-called Devil's Chapel, passed early in the walk, is part of the scowles, or workings, from which ore was extracted in Roman — and possibly pre-Roman times.

Stone-quarrying is another ancient Forest industry, and one which continues at the present time. Pennant sandstone was used in the construction of the Severn Tunnel, Berkeley Power Station and University College, London. The site of the iron foundry passed at Bream stands in an old quarry and others can be seen on other Forest Walks described in the book.

Among the more prominent relics of the Dean's industrial past are the tramways and railways that served to transport the coal and iron from the mines to the major dispersal points. Examples encountered on the walk include the stone sleepers — with the holes by which the rails were attached still visible — along the walk from Mill Hill to Noxon Park, and the bed of the standard-gauge railway walked along immediately afterwards and again later towards Parkend.

The recently-abandoned twin-adit coal mine by the side of the dismantled railway near Noxon Park is typical of those still working in the Forest. The first mines were worked from shallow outcrops during Roman times but by the 13th century the right of 'Free mining' had been established, by which a Forester (a man born in the Hundred of St. Briavels) could, after serving an apprenticeship of a year and a day, register with the Gaveller (The King's Warden) and in so doing be able to work his own gale anywhere in the area. Later, deeper seams were worked by colliery companies who sank shaft mines, the last of which closed in 1965.

The most extensive industrial relic passed on the route is Darkhill Furnace, built by the Scottish iron-master David Mushet early in the 19th century and recently partly restored. Here, refined iron was produced by newly-discovered processes.

Parkend was a major centre throughout the prime years of the Forest's industrial prosperity. Coal pits, iron and tin works, lime kilns and tramroads were scattered everywhere around and the railway, complete with station, further signified its importance. By 1908, however, the works had been closed, the chimneys had gone and only Castlemain Colliery (the site of which is passed on the forestry walk) remained. Today, the sole reminder of the boom years is the splendid blowing-engine house, now serving as a field study centre.

The later stages of the walk provide views of a tree-clad colliery tip near Whitecroft and of two small working adit mines at Parkhill and Brockhollands.

Route directions
Walk towards Bream and go through the gap to the right of a gate marked

Chelfridge on the left. Ignore a track on the left. The scowles soon come into view, chiefly on the right of the track, including the Devil's Chapel (like the other scowles, on private land). Where the track ends, at the foot of a slope, turn right, passing over two stiles, to follow a hedge on the right along a field. A third stile leads to a track which climbs to a lane. Turn right along it to reach Bream, opposite the church.

Turn left along the pavement, passing the Old Winding Wheel Inn (informative inn-sign). Just past the de-restriction sign, turn right beyond a cottage to follow a track, passing the site of an old iron foundry in a quarry on the left. The track soon veers to the right, crosses a road, and passes a bungalow on the left to reach another road. Keep on along this road, following yellow arrows. When the road bends to the right, descend a track into woodland.

On reaching a road at Mill Hill, turn left along it, and in 40 yards turn left again along a narrow track with stone walls on either side. This was the line of a tramway – notice the stone sleepers. Keep left at a cottage. The walk soon joins a dismantled railway line and passes an abandoned twin-adit coal mine on the right. On reaching a large clearing, keep right to cross a stile alongside a gate. Follow the broad woodland path through Noxon Park, leaving the wood by a stile. Cross a field, keeping a ditch and bushes on the left. At a narrowing in the field, turn sharp right up a bank under beeches. When the trees end on the left, cross a stile on the left into another field. Follow the left-hand edge to pass through a gateway. In the next field, turn right along the hedge and strike out across the field, following a line of trees to reach a stile by a metal gate. Turn right along the B4228 to reach the Orepool Inn.

From the inn, keep on along the B4228 as far as a road fork. Bear right here and follow this road through the village of Sling. After passing the entrance to a lorry park on the left, watch out for a marker stone also on the left and follow the path by it through woodland to reach a road opposite a house. Turn left, then immediately right to follow the garden fence to reach a track into woodland. Dip to cross a stream and at a cross track, turn right and climb to reach a power pole (numbered XSG 49). Turn left here to follow the curve of a dismantled railway. The remains of Mushet's Darkhill furnaces can be seen on the left. Descend the embankment to cross the B4431 and climb to join the old line once more, following it past quarries and through a cutting as far as a T-junction, beyond which stands a works at the approach to Parkend.

Turn right here to join the B4431 and then left into Parkend. After seeing the village, and especially the engine house of the former furnaces (now a field-study centre), retrace steps along the B4431 as far as the drive on the left signposted Whitemead Park. Follow this as far as a cattle grid at the Park entrance, then bear right up a track, crossing two stiles, to meet another track. Turn right along it and in about 70 yards turn off left to climb a grassy path into Parkhill Inclosure. This path soon dips and eventually reaches a junction of several paths at a clearing. Take the fourth track from the left (i.e. the right-hand of two straight ahead). Cross a stile by a gate (wooded pit tip on right) and keep on down a track to pass Parkhill Lodge and reach Whitecroft.

Cross a road (Royal Oak Inn on left) and follow another road, which swings to the right past Parkhill mine and climbs to a junction with a minor road coming in from the right at Brockhollands. The road now dips and in the hollow, opposite the lane to Tufts Fish Farm, turn right into woodland, passing a small coal mine on the right. Climb steadily along the woodland path as far as ruined buildings. Here the path swings to the left and climbs steeply, before levelling off and becoming somewhat ill-defined as it approaches the road ahead. Turn right along the verge back to the layby.

The Buckstone, Staunton

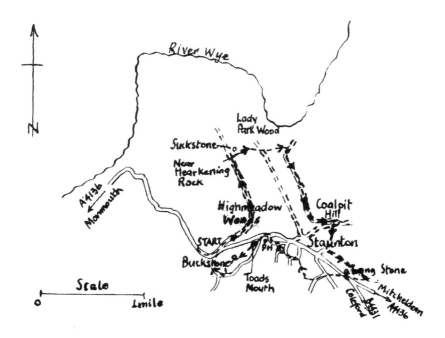

Walk 5
Another part of the Forest — Stones and scenery near Staunton

Theme: The origins of and legends associated with some of the stones
in the scenic western area of the Forest of Dean.

Start and finish: Layby on right hand side of A4136, approx. a mile
west of Staunton.

Getting there: Staunton (note: the Forest village of this name) lies on
the A4136, approx. 3 miles northwest of Coleford and approx. 4
miles east of Monmouth.

Route of walk: A4136 layby — Highmeadow Woods — Suckstone —
Near Hearkening Rock — Lady Park Wood — Coalpit Hill — Long
Stone — Staunton — Toad's Mouth Rock — Buckstone — Layby.

Distance: 6¼ miles.

Summary of terrain: Good woodland paths most of the way. Some steep
gradients, especially up to Near Hearkening Rock.

O.S. Sheet: Landranger 162 — Gloucester and Forest of Dean. (1¼
inches to 1 mile).

Starting point grid ref: 538124.

Parking: Layby off A4136 (see above).

Refreshments: White Horse Inn, Staunton.

Recommended reading: Secret Forest. Ray Wright, Forest Bookshop,
Coleford, 1980.

Theme

Gloucestershire has two Stauntons. The Forest Staunton lies on the
Mitcheldean-Monmouth road on the western extremity of both county
and forest and its name — said to have been derived from stane, or stone
— could hardly be more appropriate, for within walking distance of the
village can be seen several impressive stones.

With the exception of the Long Stone, all these stones are natural
features, fashioned into their present state over millions of years by natural
weathering. They are composed of what is known as quartz conglomerate,
a mixture of the local Old Red Sandstone and quartz pebbles and appear
as gigantic boulders.

The first stones encountered on the walk — The Suckstone and Near
Hearkening Rock — lie in Highmeadow Woods, part of a large estate
acquired by the Crown in 1817. The Suckstone is a huge, wedge-shaped
rock, perched on a steep slope, on to which it must have fallen countless
centuries ago. It is believed to be the largest single block of stone in
the country but theories on its weight — like those on the origins of its
name — vary considerably, ranging from 4,000 to 14,000 tons.

Both the Near Hearkening and Far Hearkening Rocks (the latter lies off the walk) — are reputed to have got their names from the the ability of people listening there to receive messages transmitted through the earth from the Buckstone, the celebrated rocking stone, a mile away to the south. A more likely explanation is that gamekeepers concealed themselves beneath the overhanging rock listening for the approach of poachers.

The next stone encountered on the walk is the Long Stone, the only ancient stone of human origin around Staunton. It stands — or rather leans — some 7 feet high by the side of the Mitcheldean-Monmouth road and is believed to date from Bronze Age times, when it may have been a marker stone for a cemetery. A combination of weathering and vandalism has marked the stone considerably but it is still an impressive sight and it is understandable why many stories are associated with it, including one that if pricked with a pin at midnight on the summer solstice it will bleed!

Jutting out over the road to Monmouth is the so-called Toad's Mouth rock. It is easy to see why this rock formation is so called, although the imaginative may well consider that this result of much weathering resembles a larger, fiercer beast! Again, local legend associates a stone with the shedding of blood — this time that of lawbreakers in prehistoric times, who were said to have been beheaded in a depression on the flat top of the rock.

A good walk saves at least one of its finest sights until near the end and this is no exception. The Buckstone commands splendid views and is worthy of seeing as yet another interesting rock formation. Before 1885, however, the Buckstone was a delicately-poised rocking stone, balancing on an apex of a mere 3 feet in circumference, and could be vibrated, according to one report, by 'The united force of two or three pairs of broad shoulders.' In that year, however, a party of irresponsible men from Monmouth succeeded in toppling the Buckstone from its place and it is now fixed permanently by concrete and an iron pin.

Route Directions

From the layby, walk along the road towards Staunton. Just before a 'Parking 1 mile' sign, turn left along a woodland track into Highmeadow Woods, running roughly parallel to the road. When this track sweeps to the left, turn right along another track, which in turn soon veers left, giving good views westwards. Eventually, after about a mile, the large flat Suckstone is reached, standing on the slope on the right. (Yellow arrows now mark the way). Climb up to the stone and take the steep path to the right, passing several smaller rocks, to reach the vast Near Hearkening Rock. Turn left in front of it and follow the path, climbing up above the rock. This path soon swings away to the left through the trees to reach a forest road. Cross this road and take a narrow path between the trees, which soon dips and reaches a T-junction of paths. Turn left here to meet the forest road once more at Lady Park National Nature Reserve.

Continue the descent straight ahead, ignoring yellow arrows indicating left by the edge of the nature reserve, as far as a wide forest road at the bottom of the slope. Turn right along this road and climb steadily for about a mile to a four-lane-ends of tracks where the road levels. On the left is tree-clad Coalpit Hill and a caravan park, also on high ground nearby. Turn right here, crossing a stream and passing a barrier. In 100 yards, just before a power pole, turn left along a narrow woodland path. Climb beyond two cross tracks to meet a wide curving track at the top of the slope. Turn left along it to a cross track at the top of a rise. Turn right here and right again in 100 yards at another cross track to reach the A4136 at the Long Stone.

Cross the road and follow the footpath (yellow arrow) leading through the woods slightly to the right. At a junction of forest roads, go straight across. Approaching the top of the slope, bear right along a track between conifers to a junction of tracks. Turn right and follow this track out of the woods down to its junction with a lane. Staunton can be seen ahead. Turn left, passing Kiln Cottage on the left and a barn on the right. Turn right and climb to a T-junction. After turning left along the road (signposted Monmouth), swing right by a postbox and reach the A4136. The White Horse Inn is immediately on the left.

From the inn, walk for a short way along the Monmouth road before taking the first minor road on the left. The Toad's Mouth Rock formation is about 50 yards along on the right. To reach the Buckstone, follow the lane as far as as gate with a speed-restriction sign and turn right to climb a narrow path through the bracken. After a short climb, the top of an underground reservoir appears on the left. The Buckstone is a short distance to the right, below a triangulation pillar.

To return to the car, continue along the path for a short way to a fork. Take the right fork, signposted Redbrook. At a lane by Buckstone Lodge, turn right and right again along another lane. This ends at a fork to two houses. From the left fork, ending at a gate, turn right along a descending path. When a stone wall ends on the right, turn right along a narrow path by a power pole, keeping a wall on the right. Ignore side paths. When a conifer wood appears on the left ahead, turn left downhill. The sound of traffic below indicates the close proximity of the road, which is reached through the trees. The layby is across the road on the left.

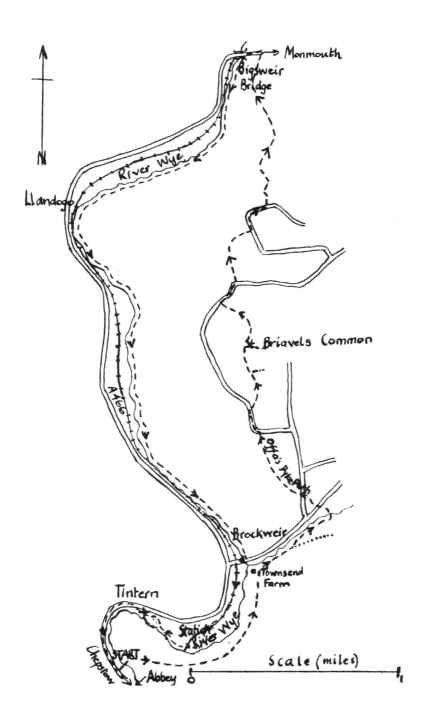

Monmouth

Bigsweir
Bridge

River Wye

Llandogo

St. Briavels Common

A466

Otto's Pyke Path

Brockweir

Townsend
Farm

Tintern

Station
River Wye

Chepstow
START
Abbey

N

Scale (miles)

Sweet chestnuts, near Bigsweir Bridge

Walk 6

Westwards to the Wye — Along the Offa's Dyke Path

Theme: Gloucestershire's section of the Wye Valley, as seen from the Offa's Dyke long-distance footpath.

Start and finish: The footbridge near Abbey Mill, Tintern.

Getting there: Tintern — Townsend Farm, Brockweir — Offa's Dyke Path — St. Briavels Common — Bigsweir Bridge — Riverside path — Brockweir Bridge — Tintern Station — Tintern.

Distance: 9 miles.

Summary of terrain: A mixture of easy riverside walking and some very steep climbs and ascents between Brockweire and Bigsweir Bridge. Approach to Townsend Farm very muddy.

O.S. Sheets: Strongly recommended: Outdoor Leisure 14 — Wye Valley and Forest of Dean (2½ inches to 1 mile).

Sheet 162 — Gloucester and Forest of Dean (1¼ inches to 1 mile).

Starting point grid ref: 530003.

Parking: Choice of car parking at Tintern — by river and at Abbey.

Refreshments: No refreshments available on route. Choice of cafes and inns in Tintern.

Recommended reading: The Wye Valley. E.J. Mason, Hale, 1987.
The Wye Valley. Richard Sale, Wildwood, 1984.

Lines composed a few miles above Tintern Abbey. William
Wordsworth, 1798.

Theme

From Lower Lydbrook to Beachley, Gloucestershire has a half-share in
the River Wye, whose valley ranks among the most scenic and unspoilt
in the whole of Britain.

Associated with the river northwards from Sedbury Cliffs, near
Chepstow, close to the confluence of the Wye with the Severn, is Offa's
Dyke, a great earthwork constructed in the 8th century AD by King Offa,
ruler of the Saxon kingdom of Mercia. Offa's Dyke marked the western
boundary of his kingdom, and extended for almost 170 miles northwards
to reach the Irish Sea near Prestatyn. It consisted of a ditch on the west
side flanked by a 20-foot mound built with the excavated earth and may
have served either in a defensive role or simply as a frontier. (The present
boundary between England and Wales lies largely along it).

The Offa's Dyke long-distance footpath was opened in 1971. Although,
like the Dyke itself, it extends from Sedbury Cliffs to Prestatyn, only
60 miles lie along the line of the actual Dyke.

Further confusion can arise in this section as the path has two roughly-
parallel courses — one along the Dyke, followed on the outward route,
and the return path along the river.

The walk begins and ends at Tintern, on the Gwent side of the Wye,
known to millions for the enchanting ruins of its 12th century Cistercian
abbey. In 1789, William Wordsworth returned here after a five year
absence to write his immortal 'Lines':

'Once again
Do I behold these steep and lofty cliffs,
That on a wild secluded scene impress
Thoughts of a more deep seclusion; and connect
The Landscape with the quiet of the sky.'

But Tintern has known industrial ugliness too. It was, according to
a plaque in the Abbey car park, the birthplace of the British brass industry,
and a tinplate works was established in 1880. Even now, the bridge over
which the walk begins is referred to as the Wireworks Bridge — a
reminder that it once carried a tramway to a wiremaking factory. Today,
the only link with Tintern's industrial past is the old railway station, passed
through on the last stages of the walk, and which is now maintained by
enthusiasts.

Few walks can compare with this for variety of scenery and wildlife.
The climb along the Dyke from beyond Townsend Farm over St. Briavel's
Common is both long and demanding but the landscape of tiny fields

intersected by winding lanes and scattered with small farms and isolated cottages is totally unlike any other to be seen in Gloucestershire. The way is lined by ancient species-rich hedges, along which wild flowers thrive. Here can be found wood sorrel and wood anemone, bluebell and bedstraw, sweet violet and great stitchwort — and many, many more flowering plants to delight the walker throughout the year.

Bird life abounds. The woods offer treecreepers, tits and woodpeckers. The hedges are favoured by blackcaps, thrushes and bullfinches, while by the riverside, good views can be had of mute swans, cormorants and wild duck. High above, a buzzard or raven may well drift into view to complete the picture.

Of the mammals, rabbits, foxes, badgers and fallow deer are well established, as also — despite attempts at control — is that enemy of the forester, the alien grey squirrel.

Route Directions

Cross the footbridge and follow the yellow arrows to the right, climbing a stone-paved track. At the top of the slope, bear left at a fork, following the Brockweir signpost through woodland. Leave the woods through a gate and keep on along a track. Beyond a gate at Townsend Farm, turn right along a track signposted Devil's Pulpit. Midway up the slope, follow a footpath sign on the left, crossing a sloping field to a stile. Cross this and a second stile into woodland. On leaving the wood, turn left along the side of a field to cross a stile and footbridge and so reach the Offa's Path (O.D.P.), which is well signposted throughout.

The path leads through woodland to a road. Turn right and immediately left. Cross a brook by a bridge. Climb to another road. Turn left and immediately right. Climb a track, crossing another road. At the next road, follow the O.D.P. to the left, climbing steadily. Take a right fork, after which the lane reverts to a narrow footpath. Ignore a stile on the right by 3 stop-valves and keep climbing to a T-junction of paths. Follow the yellow arrow to the left and climb to a lane.

Turn left here and watch closely for yellow arrows through small fields by a farm to reach a lane. Turn right and climb before dipping left along a track at a bend. The descent continues left at a road, which winds towards a large house. The O.D.P. drops to the left just before the house, descending into a steep-sided wooded valley. Leave the wood by a stile and descend a sloping field between ancient sweet-chestnut trees to another stile. The path now descends to the left by a wall, passes through a gate in a fence and then crosses a field diagonally to the right to a cattle grid. Follow the drive to meet the A466 at the approach to Bigsweir Bridge.

Just before the bridge, cross a stile on the left to follow the River Wye for 3 miles downstream to Brockweir Bridge. After crossing this bridge, go over a stile on the left and when the path forks, bear right along the dismantled railway line, passing Tintern station. Descend steps on the right down to the river and complete the walk by passing through St. Michael's churchyard to reach Tintern. The Abbey, bridge and car parks are straight ahead.

St. Mary's old church, Kempley

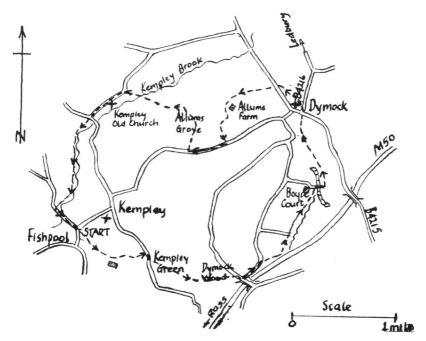

Walk 7

Border country — Dymock and the Daffodil Way

Theme: An introduction to the pleasant countryside along the Herefordshire border around the village of Dymock, famous for its wild daffodils and for its association with a group of eminent poets.

Start and finish: The hamlet of Fishpool, near Kempley.

Getting there: Fishpool lies 3 miles SW of Dymock and 3 miles north of Exit 3 on the M50 (4 miles east of Ross-on-Wye).

Route of walk: Fishpool — Kempley Green — Dymock Wood — Allums Farm — Allums Grove — St Mary's (Kempley old church) — Fishpool.

Distance: 8 miles.

Summary of terrain: Easy walking throughout. Some muddy patches after rain. Electric fences provided with rubber strips at crossing places.

O.S. Sheet: Landranger 149 — Hereford, Leominster and surrounding area (1¼ inches to 1 mile).

Starting point grid ref.: 667294.

35

Parking: Limited parking on grass verge above phone box at Fishpool.
Refreshments: Beauchamp Arms and Crown Inn, Dymock.
Recommended reading: Daffodil Way leaflet, Countryside Commission, 1988.

Theme

> 'From Marcle way,
> From Dymock, Kenpley, Newent, Bromsberrow,
> Redmarley, all the meadowland daffodils seem
> Running in golden tides to Ryton Firs.'

Until Lascelles Abercrombie came to live near Dymock and wrote these lines, daffodils had been the exclusive poetical preserve of William Worsworth. However, the wild daffodil, smaller, paler, and – in the opinion of many – more lovely than its cultivated cousins, had long been a feature of this Gloucestershire-Herefordshire borderland and demand for its delicate blooms in distant towns was great. According to another poet, Ledbury-born John Masefield, those who picked the spring blooms were:

> 'Hard-featured women, weather-beaten brown,
> Or Swarthy-red, the colour of old brick.

During the flowering season, Dymock daffodils were sent away by the trainload. They appeared to withstand all the picking and their future seemed as assured as that of the permanent way itself. The railway has long since gone from Dymock and with it the trade in wild daffodils. Though nowadays much depleted in numbers, the flowers still survive. Modern agriculture methods, rather than overpicking, have been largely responsible for the flower's decline however, and although there is little danger of it disappearing altogether, the heyday of the wild daffodil is a thing of the past.

The daffodil is not the only claim to fame of this pleasant border country. The arrival of Lascelles Abercrombie in 1911 saw the beginning of the short, yet amazingly fertile, period of the so-called 'Dymock Poets'. For the next three years, up until the outbreak of the First World War, the Dymock area became the home of such celebrated poets as Wilfrid Gibson, Edward Thomas and Robert Frost, who were visited at regular intervals by Rupert Brooke, John Drinkwater and Eleanor Farjeon. It was here that Frost convinced Edward Thomas that in poetry, rather than prose, lay his literary destiny, and it was over these fields and through these woods that the poets wandered and found much of their inspiration.

The so-called Daffodil Way that the walk follows was established in 1988, on the initiative of the Windcross Public Paths Project, and is a waymarked eight-mile circular walk offering plenty of interest in an area where footpaths generally are few and far between. Among the features of special attraction is the village of Dymock, where in the parish church can be seen a permanent display about the 'Dymock Poets'. Dymock also contains some rare examples of early timber-framed houses, as well as the White House, birthplace in 1637 of John Kyrle, the 'Man of Ross' — benefactor of the nearby Herefordshire town.

Undoubtedly the most remarkable building on the route is the 12th-century church of St. Mary, standing remote on a lane near Kempley. The village was sited nearby until persistent flooding drove the villagers uphill, leaving behind a church enriched by an amazing collection of frescoes and wall-paintings, which were not re-discovered until 1872 and were restored as recently as 1955.

This comparatively unknown corner of Gloucestershire has seen many changes since the poets and the wild daffodils thrived all those years ago. Yet despite the loss of the hedges, and the application of modern farming techniques in the fields, the woods and streams remain to delight the walker. Even the close proximity of the M50 during one stage of the walk fails to break the spell of this gentle countryside, where Gloucestershire and Herefordshire meet.

Route directions
Walk past the turn to Much Marcle on the right. In 50 yards, cross a stile on the left marked with a yellow arrow and black dot (Daffodil Way symbol). Keep hedges on the right over three stiles. In the next field, aim slightly to the right of a red-roofed white cottage (Moor House) and cross a footbridge. Pass the cottage boundary on the right and go through a gateway and over two fields to a double stile. Climb the left-hand edge of a field and when it widens, keep straight on to reach Kempley Green through a gate.

Turn right along the road and at the end of the village, just before a bungalow (Knapp View), turn left and take the right of two signposted footpaths. Cross two stiles and climb past barns on the left before descending through a gate into an orchard. Enter Dymock Wood over a stile and follow the yellow arrows through to meet a road. Turn right along it and then left just before the bridge over the motorway. When this road bends to the left, leave it through a gate and keep straight on parallel to the motorway through gates down to a stream.

Turn left along the stream and follow it, crossing a farm track by two stiles. Go through a gate to reach a track and turn left along it, following it past a lake and Boyce Court to a T-junction. Turn right here over a bridge and then left over a stile, following the stream over fields and up to Dymock, reaching the village opposite the Beauchamp Arms.

The walk continues through the churchyard. Follow the main path between the trees as far as a left bend. Keep straight on here through a kissing gate and veer left over a field to cross a footbridge. Keep a hedge on the left to reach a length of old road over a stile. Turn right along it to cross the B4215 and follow the signposted track opposite. When this track veers to the left to Allums Farm, keep straight on, with the hedge on the right. At the end of a large barn, turn half-left and pass a water trough on the left to enter an orchard through a gate.

Walk the length of the orchard, keeping first a hedge, then a fence, on the left. Leave the orchard over a stile and keep to the left-hand edge of a field to reach a road through a gate. Turn right along it and in a third of a mile take a signposted footpath on the right at a dip in the road. Keep a wood on the left for 100 yards as far as a marker post. From here, veer half-right up a gentle slope to cross a footbridge and a stile and enter Allums Grove.

Turn right in the wood, keeping a fence on the right as far as a stile on the right. Leave the wood here, turning left and keeping the wood on the left as far as another stile. Re-enter the wood, turning left and following the yellow arrows. Leave the wood through a metal handgate and cross a field, passing to the left of a pond and a ruined farmhouse to enter a field over a ditch. Follow the hedge on the right to cross a footbridge over Kempley Brook. Cross the next field half-left, aming for a stile in line with a brick cottage. Continue on this line to meet a road.

Turn left along the road to pass St. Mary's Church. At a T-junction go through a gate ahead into a field and keep straight on, passing a power pole to reach a gate. Keep the brook on the left through four fields to meet a road. Turn left along it to reach a road fork at Fishpool. The phone box is along the road on the left.

Tewkesbury

Walk 8

Tewkesbury — a town and country tour.

Theme: Tewkesbury — its history, its sights, its literary associations
and its character.

Start and finish: The main road (A38) outside the Abbey.

Getting there: Tewkesbury lies at the junction of the A38 and the A438.
Exit 9 (M5) is 1½ miles east.

Route of walk: The Abbey — The Bloody Meadow — the Baptist Chapel
— Abbey Mill and tithe barn — the Ham — Avon Lock — King
John's Bridge — Beaufort Bridge — Mythe Waterworks and Bridge
— The Mythe — High Street — the Abbey.

Distance: 8 miles.

Summary of terrain: Easy throughout. Ham and Mythe areas impassable
at times of flood. Footpath through Waterworks subject of
controversy (see route description).

O.S. Sheet: Landranger 150 — Worcester and the Malverns. (1¼ inches
to 1 mile).

Starting point grid ref: 890325.

Parking: Choice of paid and free car parks.

Refreshments: Choice of inns and cafes.

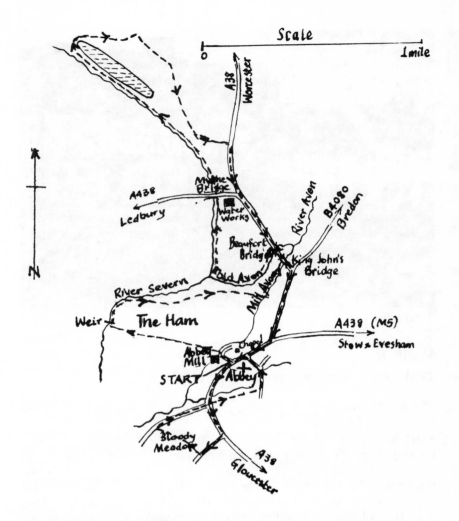

Recommended reading: Tewkesbury. Anthea Jones, Phillimore, 1987. Six English Towns. A. Chifton Taylor, BBC, 1978. Brensham Trilogy. John Moore, Collins, 1948.
Recommended to visit: Town Museum, 64 Barton Street. John Moore Museum, Church Street. Little Museum, 45 Church Street.

Theme

Tewkesbury is one of that small and select group of towns that are generally regarded as being among the best examples of their kind in England. Although close to the Cotswolds, it is a town of timber-framing and mellow brick — its one distinctive stone building being its superb Norman Abbey.

Built in the form of the letter Y, Tewkesbury stands at the confluence of the Rivers Severn and Avon, which together with the River Swilgate and the Carrant Brook, have had the effect of restricting its spread. Flooding along this part of the Severn valley has always played an influential part in Tewkesbury's life and but for its bridges — themselves a subject worthy of study — the town's development would have stultified.

Instead however, Tewkesbury has a long history of industrial enterprise. Milling, brewing and stocking-knitting flourished in the 18th and 19th centuries and new industries have been successfully established in and near the town since. Tewkesbury was also well known for its coaching traffic — it was not mere chance that had Charles Dickens bringing Mr. Pickwick to stay at the Hop Pole Hotel — but the railway was routed outside the town and this helped to preserve it from the kind of development that spoilt so many similar market towns.

The route of this walk is intended to serve as an introduction to an exploration of Tewkesbury. Much that is of interest has had to be left out — a whole day could profitably be spent around the town, omitting the Battle Trail and the Mythe altogether — but as this book is intended primarily as a guide to country walking, a blend of town and country seemed appropriate here. No visitor should miss seeing the Abbey, however, so this serves as the starting point for the walk.

Tewkesbury Abbey was built in the 12th century as a Benedictine monastery. It is by far the oldest building in the town and its handsome tower and awe-inspiring West front rank among the finest examples in the whole of England. The interior is filled with splendid tombs and fine decorative workmanship — saved like the rest of the building by the townspeople who at the dissolution of the monasteries, paid Henry VIII the sum of £453 to preserve the doomed abbey for use as their parish church.

The Bloody Meadow was the scene, on 4th May 1471, of the Battle of Tewkesbury, at which the Yorkist forces under Edward IV defeated the Lancastrians of Queen Margaret, and in doing so brought to a savage end the so-called Wars of the Roses. The eighteen-year-old Prince of Wales and Edmund Beaufort, Duke of Somerset, were among those who lost their lives in the resulting carnage, which saw the house of York's fortunes attain the prosperity that was to last until Richard III's ignominious death at Bosworth Field in 1485.

The brief detour to see the Baptist chapel and graveyard of 1623 serves also to reveal one of Tewkesbury's appealing features — the narrow alleys that abound throughout the town. Many of the these provide glimpses of the backs of some of the older properties, difficult to see from the main streets.

The Bell Inn and Abbey Mill are of literary as well as historical interest. In 'John Halifax, Gentleman', Miss Mulock (later Mrs. Craik) made use of both buildings in the setting of this popular Victorian novel. But it is the works of a 20th century writer and local man, John Moore, that best capture the atmosphere of bygone Tewkesbury. His so-called Brensham Trilogy of the 1940s, as well as several of his later works, provide entertaining as well as richly informative background reading.

The Mythe area offers a welcome diversion from town exploration. Telford's fine single-span bridge of 1826 should not be missed. The old railway line nearby is now a nature reserve, rich in plant and bird life.

Route Directions

Cross the A38 and turn left. Keep on this road to pass the Council Offices. Just beyond, turn right along Lincoln Green Lane. A Battle Trail sign indicates a field on the right, with a descriptive panel giving details of the battle. This field is Bloody Meadow. Follow the path over the field to meet a road. Turn right along it back to the A38. Cross and follow yellow arrows across a sports field, keeping close to the bank of the River Swilgate. The Abbey can be viewed well from here. The trail goes right at the road but our route turns left here along Gander Lane back to the A38.

Cross the road once more and again turn left. The intriguing little Baptist chapel and burial ground can be seen up a blind alley on the right. Beyond this, just before reaching the Bell Inn, turn right along Mill Street. The old Abbey Tithe Barn is on the left of Abbey Mill. Cross the mill bridge into Tewkesbury Ham. Go over this large meadow to the weir and turn right along the Severn bank. Near the confluence of the Severn and Avon, follow the field path to cross a footbridge by Healing's Mill. Turn left and left again over the bridge to the mill. Turn right in front of the mill entrance to cross Avon Lock and reach the A38 at King John's Bridge.

Turn left over Beaufort Bridge and cross a stile just beyond it to follow the riverside path. This enters Mythe Waterworks over a stile and leaves through a door under Mythe Bridge. (This stretch of the path has been the subject of dispute between ramblers and the water authority and the position remains unresolved at the time of writing. Should the door beneath Mythe Bridge be locked, a polite enquiry should be made at the waterworks office).

After leaving the waterworks, turn left, following the footpath sign along the river. Cross 3 stiles, passing first an osier bed and then a stretch of open water on the right. After crossing the stile at the end of this open water, turn right and go over another stile leading into a large meadow. Head half-left to cross a ditch by a gated bridge and turn right over another field. At the far corner of this field, cross a stile into the Mythe Nature Reserve. (The old railway embankment is on the left). When the track forks, take the left fork and climb a lane, passing above the entrance to a railway tunnel and eventually reaching the A38.

Turn right, cross, and follow the pavement back to Tewkesbury entering the town at the bottom of High Street. The Abbey is on the left beyond the junction at the centre of the town.

Coal House Inn, Apperley

Walk 9

The Coombe Hill Canal — Carrying coals to Cheltenham

Theme: Tracing the route taken by coal barges supplying Cheltenham
and nearby villages in the 19th century. The route also provides
the opportunity to note changes that have taken place in the area
since the decline of coal traffic.

Start and finish: Coombe Hill canal wharf.

Getting there: Coombe Hill canal wharf lies ¼ mile north-west of the
traffic lights at the junction of the A38 with the A4019, 4 miles
north-west of Cheltenham.

Route of walk: Coombe Hill canal wharf — canal towpath — Wainlode
— Haw Bridge — Coal House Inn — Apperley — canal wharf.

Distance: 7 miles.

Summary of terrain: Easy level walking throughout. Canal towpath
can be impassable after heavy rain and Coal House Inn flooded.
Paths between Apperley and Coombe Hill may be obscure.
Beware electric fences.

O.S. Sheets: Landranger 162 — Gloucester & Forest of Dean.
150 — Worcester & and the Malverns

Starting point grid ref: Sheet 162 — 886273

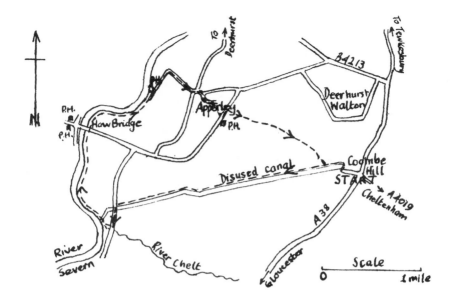

Parking: Limited parking at end of canal wharf approach lane.
Refreshments: Coal House Inn, Apperley. Farmers Arms, Apperley.
Recommended reading: Severn Tide. Brian Waters, Dent, 1947.
  (Reprinted Alan Sutton, 1987).

Theme
This walk follows the towpath of a disused canal, proceeds along a
stretch of the Severn Way long-distance path — passing a couple of
interesting pubs — climbs to the village of Apperley and returns to the
start over fieldpaths.

The reference to coal in the title relates to the historical origins of the
canal and also of a wharf and one of the inns on the route. The Coombe
Hill canal was constructed between the years 1796-1797 to enable coal
from the Forest of Dean and South Wales coalfields to be transported
to the expanding town of Cheltenham. It was a short waterway — only
2½ miles long — and linked the River Severn at Wainlode with the
hamlet of Coombe Hill, 4 miles north-east of the town, where the coal
was transferred from the canal boats to horse-drawn wagons.

As the canal was dug over the flat, low-lying landscape of the Chelt
Valley, no locks were needed, apart from the double entrance lock still
visible at the junction with the river. On the face of it, such a short
broad-width canal should have proved a successful venture but this was
not to be the case. Winter flooding was a problem from the outset, but

45

competition — first from a horse tramway from Gloucester docks and later from the new railway — caused the canal to lose trade and to be finally abandoned in 1876.

In recent years the waterway has been acquired by the Gloucestershire Trust for Nature Conservation and the maintenance of various water and marshland habitats will in time further enhance this species-rich area by attracting additional bird, insect and plant life.

After leaving the canal towpath at Wainlode, the meeting places of the River Chelt and the canal with the Severn can both be seen before Haw Bridge is reached. This modern bridge, opened in 1961, replaced the original structure depicted on the Haw Bridge Inn sign, which was badly damaged by a runaway barge. It had been built in 1825 to replace the Haw Passage ferry with a view to facilitating a direct route linking London to Hereford via Cheltenham but this scheme never came to fruition. Remains of a wharf and associated buildings can be seen near the inn.

A further reminder of the importance of coal traffic along this section of the Severn is seen further upstream. This is the Coal House Inn, built at the site of the wharf at which coal was unloaded for Apperley and neighbouring villages. After the coal trade declined, the inn was renamed the White Lion but happily the original name has been restored.

In times of flood, the Coal House is frequently under water and cut off from Apperley on the slope above, as can be seen by a dramatic set of photographs inside the inn.

The concluding stages of the walk from Apperley back to the canal wharf at Coombe Hill entail unexceptional walking over flat agricultural land, the latter stages of which can be enlivened by the sight of waterfowl on the marshy ground alongside the canal.

Route directions

Walk along the right bank of the canal for approx 2½ miles. At a road, turn left. Just before a hump-backed bridge over the River Chelt, turn right along the Severn Way Path. Yellow arrows indicate the route along the raised bank to a stile over the canal. The junction with the Severn is a short distance on the left. Follow the Severn Way over bridges and stiles to reach a road at Haw Bridge. Continue upstream on the right bank. Pass through a caravan park to reach the Coal House Inn.

From the inn, follow the lane to Apperley. At the village cross-roads, take the road signposted 'Tewkesbury and Cheltenham'. Turn right at the first turn and at the end of road, go through a gateway and along a drive leading to a guest house. Just before the house, cross a stile by a gate on the right to enter a field. After crossing another stile in a wire fence, keep on the same line to cross a further stile in the far corner of the field. Now keep a hedge on the right and head for the Farmer's Arms Inn to reach a road over another stile in front of the inn.

Turn left along the road. Just before a house on the right, go along a drive to a stile on the left of a garage. Cross straight over a field to pass through a gateway. Cross the next field on the same line and go over two stiles on either side of a newly-planted wood. The next field is a large arable one. Cross it to reach a track at right angles just past a dried-up pond on the left surrouned by trees.

From now on the route at the time of writing was difficult to trace because of erased paths, missing stiles and the removal of a footbridge following ditching. The actual route crosses the field ahead almost on the line of the large oak tree in the next-but-one field . . . passing through an overgrown metal gate in the hedge on the line. However, it may be thought preferable to turn right along the track and follow it round as far as an oak tree at the extremity of a hedge on the left. In this case, pass the tree and keep the hedge on the left for 100 yards to reach the overgrown gate. From this gate, the route passes slightly to the left of the oak used for alignment purposes earlier. Ditching has caused the removal of the footbridge in the middle of this large field, however, and the following diversion may be necessary.

Keep on round the edge of this large irregular field with the hedge on the left. Do not go through a gap in the hedge at a right-hand corner at which houses can be seen ahead. Instead, follow the hedge to the end of the field — a point where two ditches meet. This is the original route. Cross two wire fences and turn left through a gate. Head out across the next field to a stile approximately half-way along the opposite hedge. Cross this stile and a plank bridge and turn right along a hedge to cross another bridge at a gap. Turn left and keep a hedge on the left as far as a gate, with Coombe Hill ahead. Go through this gate and head half-right to climb a white stile onto the canal towpath. Turn left along it back to the start.

Keble's Bridge, Eastleach

Walk 10

Bridges and boundaries — the lower Leach and upper Thames valleys

Walk 1

Theme: The lower Leach Valley — its ancient bridges, and the three lovely villages by the river.

Start and finish: Eastleach Martin church.

Getting there: The Eastleaches lie 2¼ miles west of the A361 and 3½ miles north of Lechlade.

Route of walk: Eastleach Martin — Southrop — Eastleach Martin — Eastleach Turville.

Distance: 2¼ miles.

Summary of terrain: Easy walking throughout.

O.S. Sheet: Landranger 163 — Cheltenham and Cirencester area (1¼ inches to 1 mile).

Starting point grid ref: 202052.

Parking: Eastleach Martin.

Refreshments: Swan Inn, Southrop.

Recommended reading: Thirteen Rivers to the Thames. Brian Waters, Dent, 1964.

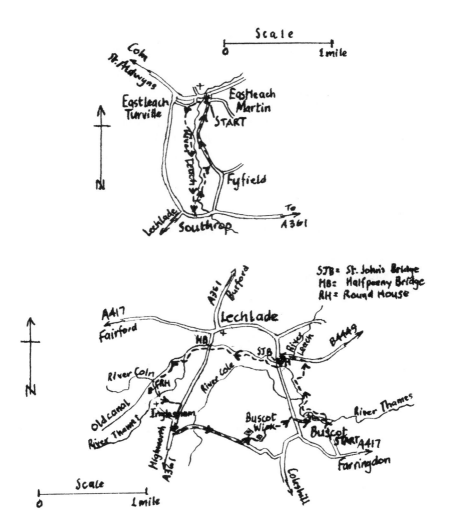

Walk 2

Theme: The confluence of the Leach and Thames and the bridges and other riverside features of this corner where Gloucestershire meets Oxfordshire and Wiltshire.

Start and finish: National Trust car park, Buscot.

Getting there: Buscot lies off the A417, 2 miles south of Lechlade.

Route of walk: Buscot – Buscot Lock – St. John's Bridge – Halfpenny Bridge, Lechlade – Inglesham – Buscot Wick – Buscot.

49

Distance: 5 miles.

Summary of terrain: Easy walking throughout though route not always obvious.

O.S. Sheet: Landranger 163 — Cheltenham and Cirencester area (1¼ inches to 1 mile).

Starting point grid ref: 232977.

Parking: National Trust car park or in Buscot village.

Refreshments: Trout Inn, St. John's Bridge. Apple Tree Inn, Buscot.

Recommended reading: Upper Thames Valley. H. Knights, 1985. The Upper Thames. J.R.L. Anderson, Methuen, 1974.

Recommended to visit: Buscot House (National Trust).

Theme

It had been intended to cover this corner of Gloucestershire — and the Wiltshire-Oxfordshire borderland where the Leach and Thames meet — during the course of one walk. Unfortunately however, some of the footpaths proved so difficult to follow that it was found necessary to describe two separate walks, both of which offer varied riverbank walking with the opportunity to study a wide range of bridges and other man-made features associated with both the use and control of rivers.

The River Leach rises in the parish of Hampnett, a mile or more north-west of Northleach — the only town along its 15-mile course and meets the Thames at Lechlade. In its lonely upper reaches this modest river is scarcely more than a stream, noted only for the quality of its watercress, but its middle reaches are remarkable for the Leach's habit of disappearing underground during the summer months.

The Eastleaches — Eastleach Turville and Eastleach Martin — are the best-known villages on the river. Apart from their beauty they are remarkable for the close proximity of their ancient churches and for the fine clapper bridge, reminiscent of those in Devon, crossed at the beginning of the walk. This is often referred to as Keble's Bridge, in honour of the family of that name, who held the manor of Eastleach Turville for several generations and from whom John Keble, author of 'The Christian Year' and curate here in the last century, was descended.

Another interesting and primitive bridge is crossed on the return stage of the walk. Notice the simple breakwaters on the upstream side. A converted water mill, with its leat, and a weir nearby on the Leach, are also passed along the road back to Eastleach.

Lechlade is the only Gloucestershire town on the River Thames. Its days as a trading port have gone but its popularity among pleasure-boating people makes it a busy place throughout the summer months. This walk skirts the town, viewing its interesting bridges and other features on the river bank and offering glimpses of the confluences of the Leach and the Coln with the Thames. The route also passes the place where the Thames and Severn Canal, long since abandoned, joins the river it once linked to the Severn across 29 Gloucestershire miles.

Those with an interest in the harnessing of rivers in the service of man will find time at Buscot Lock well spent. The original weir cottage still stands nearby. St. John's Bridge, Lechlade, dates from the 14th century. It was drastically altered in 1831 and again in 1884. Nearby, by the Thames lock, the highest on the river, stands Monti's figure of Father Thames, created for the Great Exhibition at the Crystal Palace in 1851 and erected here in 1974, after having been damaged by vandals at its former site at Thames Head.

As its name indicates, Halfpenny Bridge was once a toll bridge, and a good view is obtained of the toll-house standing beside it. This bridge opened in 1792 and the walk passes through its towpath arch.

Those with an interest in old churches may well wish to make a slight diversion to see St. John the Baptist church at Inglesham, a tiny hamlet in the corner of Wiltshire crossed on the walk. Once a priory chapel, it dates from the 13th century, and was a great favourite of William Morris, the poet and craftsman who lived at Kelmscott, over the border in Oxfordshire.

Route — Walk 1
Route directions
From the churchyard, walk along the riverside path and cross the clapper bridge. Turn left along a lane, keeping left at the war memorial and then bearing right at the phone box. At the next junction, turn left (yellow arrows), then right and finally leave the village by turning left by the tiny telephone exchange and following the footpath to cross a stile. Cross a field to a stile by a power pole and in the next field, keep a line of trees and bushes on the left to meet the Leach briefly before striking off, still with the line of trees and bushes on the left, to go through a gate to reach a finger-type signpost.

Turn half-right here, in the direction indicated by the 'Thumbs up' marker, to cross a footbridge. Go through a handgate and along the left-hand edge of a field, passing a house and ruined barns. Cross the approach track to reach a stile and cross a large field to a stile by a power pole where a field wall meets a hedge. Follow the clear path over two stiles into Southrop.

After seeing the village, retrace the outward route as far as the stile by the power pole at the meeting of a wall and a hedge. From here, leave the path to cross the Leach by a quaint little bridge. Cross a stile on the left just over the bridge and follow the river upstream before climbing up to a road. Turn left and follow the road back to Eastleach, passing Coate Mill, the mill leat, and the weir on the Leach. By crossing the road bridge, Eastleach Turville can be explored at the end of the walk.

Route — Walk 2
Route directions

Follow the lane down to Buscot Lock. Turn right along the footpath signposted Lock Cottage. Cross a lock, a bridge and a second lock and after crossing a stile, turn left along the towpath. Keep on along the meandering river bank to reach a metal handgate about 50 yards from the river, after which the route follows a grassy track to meet a road. Turn left along it, crossing the last bridge over the Leach and passing the last water mill (now a private house). Turn left along the A417 by the Trout Inn. From the parapet of St. John's Bridge, the confluence of the Leach with the Thames can be seen to the left.

Just over St. John's Bridge, go through a handgate on the right and down steps to Thames Lock. (Notice statue of Father Thames in front of lock house). Go through a gate ahead and along the Thames, passing under Halfpenny Bridge, Lechlade. Just beyond a red footbridge, the River Coln joins the Thames on the opposite bank and the silted-up entrance of the Thames and Severn Canal can be seen to the right of the round house close by. Keep on along the river and after crossing a footbridge over a small stream, leave the river, crossing a field to the left of a power pole to reach a stile on the A361.

Turn right along this busy road (no pavement). In ¼ mile, turn left along a lane signposted Buscot. In ¾ mile, turn left along a bridleway by Buscot Wick Farm. Ignore a yellow arrow indicating left. Instead turn right along a drive to go through a handgate. Pass a house on the left and cross a field to go through a metal gate. Cross a large field, aiming along the line of two large oaks, the first in the middle of the field, the other by the gate on the route. From this gate, reach the road by skirting the next field, keeping the hedge on the left.

Cross the road, following the signpost to Buscot church. Go through the churchyard and out by the lychgate. Yellow arrows indicate the path, which follows the Thames to meet the outward route near the water works. Turn right and retrace steps back to the car park.

Churchyard Cross, Ampney Crucis

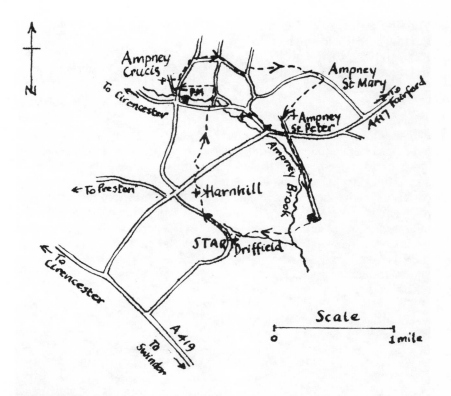

Walk 11

Churches all the way — an amble round the Ampneys.

Theme: An exploration of the villages on and near the A417, east of
Cirencester, with particular emphasis on the ancient and beautiful
churches along the route.

Start and finish: Driffield church.

Getting there: Driffield lies approx. midway between the A417 and the
A419, approx. 3½ miles SE of Cirencester.

Route of walk: Driffield — Harnhill — Ampney Crucis — Ampney St
Mary — Ampney St Peter — Driffield.

Distance: 6¼ miles.

Summary of terrain: No gradients worth speaking of. A little road
walking necessary. Some stretches of footpath obliterated by
ploughing. Electric fences near Ampney Crucis.

O.S. Sheet: Landranger 163 — Cheltenham & Cirencester area. (1¼
inches to 1 mile).

54

Starting point: grid ref: 075998.
Parking: Driffield village.
Refreshments: Crown of Crucis hotel, Ampney Crucis.
Recommended reading: Cotswold Churches. David Verey. Alan
   Sutton. 1982.

Theme

Few regions of England possess a greater variety of well-preserved old churches than the Cotswolds. The honey-coloured oolitic limestone has been fashioned with skill and beauty for close on a thousand years and although replacement, rebuilding and restoration have taken place continually since then, what remains is a rich and infinitely varied heritage of splendid churches, incorporating almost every architectural style and internal feature. A hundred or so of these Gloucestershire churches date back to Norman times; many contain substantial Saxon traces; some, such as Deerhurst, Elkstone, Duntisbourne Rouse and Fairford – are 'musts' for anyone making a serious study of the evolution of the English parish church.

But, as the church historian David Verey says in 'Cotswold Churches': 'it is not necessary to have an architectural training to enjoy what has been called 'church-crawling'...What is important is to possess some kind of historical awareness, and a sense of wonder.'

In choosing such a 'church crawl' as a theme for one of these walks, it seemed sensible to plan a walk on which several old and interesting churches could be visited within a comfortable distance. The valley of the Ampney Brook meets this requirement – five churches lie in fairly close proximity within the angle formed by the Roman Akeman Street and Ermin Way, east of Cirencester, and the attractive villages which they serve are linked by pleasant footpaths – all of which makes for good walking whether or not the theme is adhered to. The churches are described in the order in which they are encountered on the walk.

St. Mary's, Driffield: By far the least attractive of the five. As the church guide says, 'An undistinguished pile' – gaunt 18th-century tower and a 19th-century Victorian-Gothic re-building. There are a few Norman fragments but the most interesting features are the 18th-century box pews and pulpit and the oddly-worded tablets to two former lords of the manor in the chancel.

St. Michael's, Harnhill: A Norman church, though mostly rebuilt in the 13th and 14th centuries. The most outstanding feature is the tympanum over the Norman south doorway. This depicts the winged St. Michael fighting a dragon, which is described by David Verey as 'rather a jolly sort with wings, claws, curly tail and beastly head.' There are some fragments of medieval glass in the east window.

The Church of the Holy Rood, Ampney Crucis: A church containing work from every period from Saxon to Victorian. The Saxon remnant is a north doorway, visible only from inside the building. The chancel arch and font are Norman. The life-size recumbent effigies of the Lloyd family date from 1584. A fine 15th-century cross can be seen in the churchyard. Its gabled head was found walled up inside the church in 1860 and shows the Virgin Mary on one face and the Crucifixion on another.

St. Mary's, Ampney St. Mary: A little 12th-century church near the former site of the village, which was abandoned after the Black Death (c.1350). The most notable feature is the extensive wall painting — amazingly clear despite having been executed over 600 years ago. The theme is 'Keep Holy the Sabbath Day' and the detail deserves patient study.

St. Peter's, Ampney St. Peter: With its nave and tower-arch, this church contains the most Saxon work of all. The through-stones — a typical Saxon feature — can be clearly seen. The Victorian restoration by Sir George Gilbert Scott was sensitively carried out. There is a 14th-century cross in the churchyard.

Route directions:

From Driffield church, walk along the road towards Harnhill. In about ½mile, cross a ditch on the right over a stone slab bridge and climb a stile into a field. Go half-left, aiming for a dovecote, to reach a road at Harnhill through a kissing gate. Turn right along this road as far as a stile in the wall on the left, just past barns. Cross a small field to another stile and over the next field to reach a drive by the end of some buildings on the left. Harnhill church is on the left.

From the church, follow the drive to a road and turn right. Where the hedge on the left ends, cross a stile in the fence into a field. Keep the hedge on the left, following it as it bends to the right. Near the end of the field, midway between a bend in the hedge and the far corner, go through a gap in the hedge (traces of two handgates can be seen) and keep a hedge on the right to the bottom of the next field. Now go through a gap on the right and keeping on the same line, descend over a field to reach the A417 over a fence (stile missing), opposite a minor road by mill cottages.

Cross the A417 and walk along the minor road. At a fork beyond a bridge, go left and then left again along a marked footpath (in fact a track) just past Ford Farmhouse. When the track ends, cross a field straight ahead, aiming for a stile immediately to the left of the left-hand house. Cross stiles and a footbridge and pass through a sports field and a garden fringe to reach a road. Turn left and soon right for Ampney Crucis church.

Leaving the churchyard, take the footpath directly opposite the gate, cross a drive and go through a gate by an old cross to reach a road. Turn left and walk through the village. At a T-junction, turn left and just beyond the houses, turn right along a marked footpath. Keep a wall on the right as far as a corner. Then cross a field, aiming to the left of a telephone pole to cross a stiled bridge. Now keep a hedge on the right as far as a gate on the right. Go through this and another to reach a road. Turn left into Ampney St. Mary.

Keep right at a fork by a phone box and cross a stile on the right just beyond gates in a recess in a wall. Go through a handgate and over a stile. Now keep a wall on the left up a sloping field, passing a small wood on the right before going through a handgate at the top of the field to reach a junction of paths. Turn right down a track to meet a drive. Turn left. Ampney St. Peter church is on the left.

From the church, keep on to meet the A417. To see the lovely little church of Ampney St. Mary (remote from the village of the same name), it is necessary to walk for about ⅓ mile along the pavement to the right and to retrace steps. The church is on the left.

Back at the junction of the A417 with the lane to Ampney St. Peter, cross the road and follow the no-through-road for about ¾ mile. The metalled road ends at a farm. Turn right just beyond the buildings to follow a field track. In about ½ mile, Driffield church can be seen ahead. When the track swings to the left, ignore a stone stile straight on. Instead, cross a wooden bridge and turn right along the edge of a field. Keep on to pass in front of farm buildings and along the farm drive to climb a stile and so arrive back at the starting point.

Canal Roundhouse, Cerney Wick

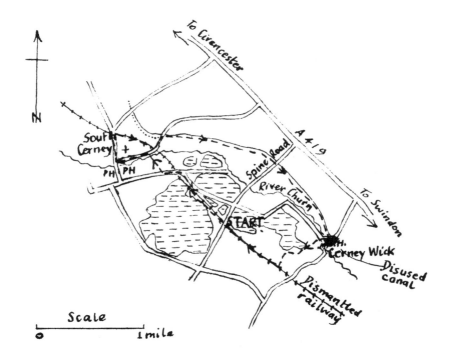

Walk 12

A changing landscape — the Cotswold Water Park.

Theme: A region where changes — in the form of a canal, a railway, gravel extraction, and the creation of a complex recreational amenity — have resulted in an environment far different from that which existed 200 years ago.

Start and finish: Official car park behind old brick railway bridge, Spine Road, near South Cerney.

Getting there: The Cotswold Water Park car park lies 1½ miles west of the A419, a mile SE of South Cerney, and 5 miles SE of Cirencester.

Route of walk: Cotswold Water Park car park — South Cerney — Thames and Severn canal — Cerney Wick — car park.

Distance: 5¼ miles.

Summary of terrain: Easy level walking throughout.

O.S. Sheet: Landranger 163 — Cheltenham & Cirencester area. (1¼ inches to 1 mile).

Starting point: grid ref: 063962.

59

Parking: Car park (see above).
Refreshments: Crown Inn, Cerney Wick.
Old George and Eliot Arms, South Cerney.
Recommended reading: Cotswold Water Park — official publicity material published by Glos. County Council, Shire Hall, Gloucester.
The Thames & Severn Canal. Humphrey Household. Alan Sutton. 1983.

Theme

The walk is routed through a flat region in the valley of the Upper Thames which for centuries was a remote farming area where cattle browsed and hay meadows buzzed with insect life in the warm days of early summer. This was a green countryside divided by hedgerows into small fields — a sight which can still be enjoyed on certain stretches of the walk.

The first change to this rustic scene took place in the 1700s, when the area was invaded by gangs of navvies drafted in to 'dig the cut'. A canal sliced through the fields linking the Severn with the Thames. In its time, this waterway, with its associated narrow boats and rough working folk, probably caused as much disturbance to what had seemed a changeless way of life as subsequent industrial invasions.

The canal had a chequered history as other waterways opened but it continued to carry local goods until the early years of the present century. The stretch along which the walk passes was finally abandoned in 1927.

One of the main reasons for the closure of the canal was the opening of the railway linking Cirencester and Swindon in 1883. This was used both for passengers and for the transporting of agricultural products, such as hay and milk. It was especially important during the two World Wars, for conveying troops from the Midlands and the North for embarkation at Southampton. The railway suffered a similar fate to that of the canal, however, and was closed finally in 1961, leaving two distinctive scars only a short distance apart across the landscape.

Fortunately, time and nature together are great healers and these relics of a bygone age now blend into the landscape, forming green corridors supporting a wealth of wildlife.

The more recent rape of this countryside has taken a different form. The soils are alluvial gravel overlying a bed of Oxford clay. The gravels have been extracted since the 1920s but only on the present vast scale since the 1960s, when new machinery was developed. These have enabled local stretches of motorway to be constructed and have also contributed greatly to the expansion of Swindon, only 12 miles distant.

An active gravel pit is an eyesore in the countryside but the County Council, since the establishment of the Cotswold Water Park, has been rigorous in landscaping the disused pits, insisting on grading of shore lines and in retention or replacement of trees. The pits have been designated for differing leisure activities and are managed accordingly. Some are used for fishing, yachting, canoeing and power-boating, while others have been landscaped to attract wildfowl. Varying stages of pool reclamation can be seen along the route, from active gravel extraction to pits where Great Crested Grebe swim in an undisturbed environment.

The car park from which the walk starts lies off Spine Road, a new road built in the 1970s to allow the heavy lorries carrying the gravel to leave the area without shattering the peace of the local villages. Two of these — South Cerney and Cerney Wick — are visited along the way. The bridge adjacent to the car park and a few other old railway bridges along the route have been retained as viewpoints, important features in such a flat landscape.

Thus the walk is routed to show the changes imposed on a rural landscape in the past 200 years. It illustrates how, with careful management, these changes need not necessarily detract from the beauty of the countryside — indeed they can enhance it and provide a wide range of facilities for a growing population.

Route directions:

From the car park, go through the gate on the right, signposted to South Cerney lakes. On reaching a road, turn left along the verge. After passing the end of Robert Franklin Way, keep on along Station Road. Just after the Lennards, follow the public footpath sign on the right over a tiny bridge. At another bridge by a converted water mill, turn left along the lane by the River Churn to reach South Cerney at Silver Street. (A sign informs us that the lane is called Bow Wow!)

Turn right along Silver Street. Immediately beyond the village sign, cross a stile on the right (just before the Driffield and Cricklade turn) and climb up to the old railway embankment. Pass through two gates. At a brick bridge, follow the well-worn path to the right and climb up to cross the bridge and continue along a lane. Watch for a footpath sign at the top of a rise. Turn right for Cerney Wick. The derelict canal soon becomes visible on the left. Cross a stile and keep on along the old towpath as far as a stile and path indicated as leading to Cerney Wick. Follow this to a road.

Cross the road to resume the footpath walk. Ignore a path on the right signposted to the River Churn. After passing a lock and a round house, turn right for Cerney Wick. At a T-junction of roads by the Crown Inn, cross a stile. After crossing a field by a cottage, the footpath is marked by posts bearing white dots and yellow arrows. At a T-junction of paths, turn right for South Cerney along the old railway. This path reaches the road opposite the car park.

Note: Gravel extraction is still taking place in the area and the shape of the pits may vary from their appearance on the sketch map.

'Horse Guards', Cirencester Park

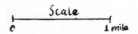

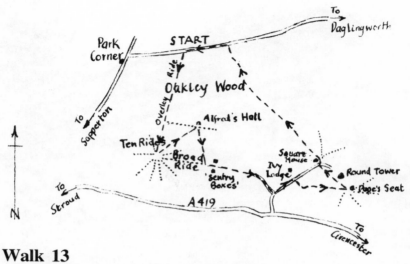

Walk 13
Oakley Wood − a park and a poet.

Theme: An 18th century park and the men who planned it.

Start and finish: On the verge on the Sapperton side of Oakley Wood (Daglingworth-Sapperton road), near to the entrance to Overley Ride. (Park Corner buildings visible ahead).

Getting there: The minor road from Daglingworth to Sapperton is approx. 2 miles north of the A419 and approx. 4 miles north-west of Cirencester.

Route of walk: Daglingworth − Sapperton road − Overley Ride − Ten Rides − Alfred's Hall − Broad Ride − Polo ground − Pope's Seat − Round Tower − Square House − Daglingworth − Sapperton road.

Distance: 6½ miles.

Summary of terrain: Easy walking throughout.

O.S. Sheet: Landranger 163 − Cheltenham and Cirencester area (1¼ inches to 1 mile).

Starting point grid ref: 967044.

Parking: grass verge.

Refreshments: Choice of inns and cafes in Cirencester.

Recommended reading: Cirencester. A History and Guide. Jean Welsford, Alan Sutton, 1987.

Gloucestershire: The Cotswolds (Buildings of England series). David Verey, Penguin, 1970

Theme

A glance at the Ordnance Survey map covering the Cotswolds reveals an extensive area of woodland crossed by rides west of Cirencester. This is Cirencester Park, containing Cirencester House, the seat of the Earls Bathurst, and described by the architect/historian David Verey as 'The finest surviving example in England of planting in the pre-landscape manner.' Oakley Wood forms the greater part of the park and it is fortunate that walkers are free to enjoy this vast area of parkland, in the creation of which the poet Alexander Pope was actively involved.

The 3,000 acre park came into being between 1704 and 1775, not as was usual, in open country, but on the edge of Cirencester itself. It owed it existence to Allen, the first Earl Bathurst, who had inherited much of the land from his father and who purchased the remainder, including Sapperton manor house, from the Atkyns family. The old manor was later demolished and its stone used in the building of various follies in the new park, several of which can be seen during the course of the walk.

One, a small pavilion known as Pope's Seat, commemorates the part played in the landscaping of the park by Alexander Pope, a close friend of Bathurst, who wrote that he was happy to: 'draw plans for houses and gardens, open avenues, cut glades, plant firs, contrive waterworks.' The Earl himself was said to be something of an expert on forestry and this interest was instrumental in ensuring that what Pope called 'the amiable simplicity of unadorned nature' — existing woods and glades — were incorporated into the overall design of the new park.

The Park's most dominant feature both on the map and on the ground is Broad Rise (or Avenue) — a vista stretching for almost five miles WNW to ESE from the Park gates on Cecily Hill to the Golden Valley at Sapperton. Of the follies — the first of their kind to be seen in this country — the walk takes in Alfred's Hall (the first English castellated mock-ruin), the Horse Guards, Ivy Lodge, The Round Tower, The Square House and Pope's Seat (already referred to). The Hexagon and Queen Anne's Monument to be viewed on another visit.

There is more to Cirencester Park than its historical associations, however. Tree lovers — naturalists of all kinds, in fact — cannot fail to find plenty to interest them. A wide range of deciduous and coniferous trees are met with during the course of the walk — some of the beeches and hornbeams are especially impressive — while the ground flora, fungi and lichens are present in rich variety in their appropriate seasons. Woodpeckers, tits, nuthatches and various species of finches favour the woodland and badgers and deer inhabit the less-frequented tracts.

The walk also provides an opportunity to see practical forestry taking place, involving felling, planting and maintenance. While for those with sporting inclinations, polo and cricket are played in what must surely be one of the most perfect settings in the whole of England.

Route directions

Walk back along the road towards Daglingworth and take the first entrance on the right into Cirencester Park (Overley Ride). The approach is broad and grassy and leads to a gate.

Important: The paths throughout this walk are concessionary — they are *not* public footpaths. No dogs are allowed. Please read the blue notice carefully before proceeding.

Walk along the ride, ignoring cross tracks. The ride is eventually joined by a surfaced track coming in from the left. Keep straight on as far as a meeting of rides known as Ten Rides — count them! Coates church tower can be seen ahead. Broad Ride is at right angles on the left and Cirencester church can be seen along it, 3½ miles distant. To reach Alfred's Hall, turn along the first path on the left from the one just walked. Go over two cross-tracks to reach the folly, just beyond a clearing. Continue the walk by following the wide grassy ride directly opposite Alfred's Hall. The second cross-track reached is Broad Ride. Turn left along it to pass between the Horse Guards — two ornamental stone structures resembling giant sentry boxes. Broad Ride eventually dips to merge with a metalled track coming in from the left. Follow this, ignoring side-turns, and go through a gate to reach a junction. Turn left, following the curving road uphill to the polo ground.

Just beyond the admission kiosk, turn right along a track, which soon swings to the left before straightening. Ivy Lodge can be seen across the polo ground and Cirencester church is once more visible ahead. Soon, first the Square House, then Round Tower, come into view on the left. On reaching a T-junction of paths, cross over, keeping on Broad Ride to reach Pope's Seat, about 300 yards distant on the left. This is the limit of the walk. Keeping woodland on the right, aim in the direction of the Square House, to pass Round Tower. On reaching a road just before the Square House, turn right and then left in 20 yards before reaching an estate gate. There follows a 1½ mile straight walk along a narrow belt of woodland before the track enters Oakley Wood once more near the road. To keep road walking to a minimum, bear left at a fork. This woodland track eventually swings to the right to reach a road. This is the Sapperton-Daglingworth road from which the walk began. Turn left to return to the car.

Doorway, Ozleworth

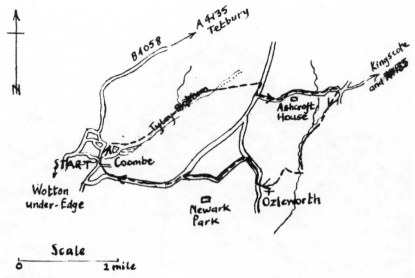

Walk 14

Gloucestershire's Deep South — A walk near Wotton

Theme: The little known, yet appealing area of the south Cotswolds east of Wotton-under-Edge, where wooded hills are dissected by tiny valleys, and roads — and the cars that clutter them — seem far away.

Start and finish: Coombe pumping station. Coombe is a mile north-east from the centre of Wotton.

Getting there: Wotton-under-Edge lies on the B4058, 5 miles south of Dursley and 12 miles west of Tetbury.

Route of walk: Coombe — Tyley Bottom — Ashcroft — Ozleworth — Newark Park — Cotswold Way — Coombe.

Distance: 6½ miles.

Summary of terrain: Undulating walking with some steep stretches. Some stiles and footbridge missing.

O.S. Sheet: Landranger 162 — Gloucester and Forest of Dean. (1¼ inches to 1 mile).

Starting point grid ref: 767938.

Parking: Limited parking by Coombe pumping station. Otherwise cars should be left along the lane from Wotton.

Refreshments: No inns on route. Choice of inns in Wotton.

Recommended reading: The Cotswolds. C. and A.M. Hadfield, Batsford, 1966.
The Cotswold Way. Mark Richards, Thornhill Press, 1984.

Theme

This delightful walk can be combined with a visit to Wotton-under-Edge, an engaging little town built on the edge of the Cotswold escarpment and an ideal place to explore in a leisurely manner. Visitors should make a point of seeing the Tolsey, the Chipping (old market place) and the 17th century Perry Almshouses. Cars can be left in the town and the starting point for the walk reached on foot (one mile), thus avoiding parking problems.

A brief glance at the area east of Wotton on the Ordnace Survey map is guaranteed to whet the appetite of any walker. Here, neatly enclosed by the B4058, the A4135 and the A46, is a region of hilly well-wooded country covering several square miles with scarcely a village in sight. A closer look reveals that the landscape is split at intervals by several east-to-west valleys, along which tiny streams trickle towards the Little Avon. It is these valleys — or bottoms as they are called locally — that give the region its special quality and it is along one of these — Tyley Bottom — that the walk begins.

Nowhere in the Cotswolds is the contrast between busy roads and quiet countryside more marked than along this lonely combe, hidden beneath the ridge, and the bustling highway running along it. Even the winds fail to penetrate to the valley floor, shielded by the hanging beechwoods, though the sun's rays fill the bottom with light. Lime-loving wild flowers grow along the way in profusion and the bird life too, is abundant, especially on the woodland fringes.

It is not until a glimpse is had of the communications tower — a smaller version of the one in London — that a jarring note of any kind mars the scene. But this is soon forgotten as the route plunges beneath the beeches once more before beginning the gentle climb to Ozleworth.

It seems appropriate that the only village passed through on this out-of-the-way (many would say out-of-this-world) walk should itself be something out of the ordinary. Ozleworth is certainly that. It consists of a Georgian house with Regency additions, a farm with an intriguing mixture of outbuildings, a few estate cottages — and a church with a central hexagonal tower, set in a circular churchyard. Add to all that the macabre morsel that the last highwayman to be hanged lies buried here, and tiny Ozleworth is well worth a leisurely inspection.

Newark Park, a National Trust property, lies alongside the later stages of the route. It stands in a fine situation at the end of a sweeping drive, built with stone from Kingswood Abbey, demolished at the Dissolution. James Wyatt carried out a drastic remodelling.

The concluding stages of the walk leave minor roads to follow the Cotswold Way — a fitting end to a delightful introduction to the sunny south Cotswolds.

Route directions

Take the public footpath signposted Tyley Bottom, which passes along a metalled drive. Leave the drive along a footpath to the left, which climbs over a stile and up a grassy bank. After passing two ponds on the right, cross another stile to reach a track. Turn right. The track eventually passes through two metal gates, with open country to the left, a stream on the right, and woods ahead. Beyond the second gate, keep right at a fork to cross another, smaller stream.

The route now passes along Tyley Bottom, following the main stream up its valley with woodland on the left. Go through a handgate into woodland and cross the stream at a favourable place (no footbridge). Keep along the right bank as far as a signposted fork in the path. Take the right fork, leaving the stream to follow blue arrows. Climb to another marker post on the hillside with woodland ahead. Follow the blue arrows through the wood and continue climbing, keeping a ruinous wall on the left to meet a track. Climb to a gate, beyond which the bridleway meets a road.

Turn right for a short distance. A communications tower looms ahead. Turn off left to pass Ashcroft Nurseries on the right and dip down to a stream. Climb the opposite bank, passing cottages, to within sight of a T-junction. Before reaching it, turn right through a gateway to the right of a small wood. The path dips between bushes to a handgate. Go through and then through a wide gateway to the left. Now descend the field, keeping a fence on the right, as far as the valley floor. Keep the stream on the right and go through a handgate alongside a field gate. The path now crosses a narrow pasture between woods and the stream. After passing through a gate the route crosses a slope above the stream.

Cross the stream by a new bridge (the original one downstream having been closed) and follow the clear track climbing to the left up to Ozleworth. Beyond the church, follow the drive, passing the great house on the left. After leaving the drive, continue straight on along the lane as far as a fork. Take the left fork, signposted Newark. Ignore side-turns and climb to pass Newark Park on the left. Keep left at a junction. Eventually, the Cotswold Way comes in from the left. The road now dips into woodland. Watch for the Cotswold Way sign on the right. Leave the road and follow it as it descends with a fence on the right to meet another road. Turn left and immediately right, back to Coombe and the start.

Norman Jewson's house, Sapperton

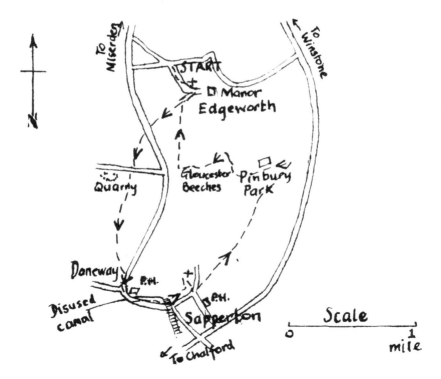

Walk 15
Cotswold craftsmen — around and about Sapperton

Theme: The lives and work of some of the most notable men in the
Cotswold art and craft movement who, in the early years of the
present century, practised their skills in the tradition established
by William Morris.

Start and finish: 'Edgeworth Church' signpost at junction of no-
through road with minor road and ½ mile east of road connecting
Miserden and Sapperton (Daneway).

Getting there: The lane to Edgeworth church lies approx. 3 miles from
both the A417 and the A419 and is 2 miles north of Sapperton and
6 miles northwest of Cirencester.

Route of walk: 'Edgeworth Church' signpost — Edgeworth —
Daneway — Sapperton — Pinbury Park — Gloucester Beeches —
Edgeworth — Church signpost.

Distance: 6½ miles.

Summary of terrain: Undulating throughout, with some fairly steep
stretches.

O.S. Sheet: Landranger 163. Cheltenham and Cirencester area (1¼
inches to 1 mile).

Starting point grid ref: 946063.

Parking: On the right, just along the lane to Edgeworth church.

Refreshments: Bell Inn, Sapperton. Daneway Inn, Daneway,
Sapperton.

Recommended reading: By Chance did I Roam. Norman Jewson,
1973.
Cotswold Crafts. Edith Brill, Batsford, 1977.

Recommended to visit: Cheltenham Museum (displays of furniture).
Arlington Mill Museum, Bibury.

Theme

The life and work of the 19th century reformer and craftsman
William Morris had a profound effect on the Cotswolds. Morris's
influence led to the founding of a Guild of Handicrafts at Chipping
Campden, involving C.R. Ashbee and F.R. Griggs, and also to a
revival of traditional styles in architecture, joinery, carving and
furniture, based at Sapperton, and featuring among others, Ernest
Gimson, the brothers Sidney and Ernest Barnsley, and later, Norman
Jewson.

Two historic houses passed on this walk — Daneway House and
Pinbury Park — featured prominently in this revival of Cotswold

craftsmanship as practised by these pioneers. Daneway House, dating from the 13th century, and the home of the Hancox family for almost 500 years, was lent by Lord Bathurst to Gimson and the Barnsleys early in the present century for use as a workshop and showroom. Here, they employed a number of local carpenters and wheelrights in the manufacture of simple yet finely-made furniture and other good-quality craft products. The workshop operated successfully until Gimson's death in 1919, after which his foreman, Peter Waals, transferred the business to Chalford, where it continued to flourish until his own death in 1938.

Pinbury Park, an ancient manor house set superbly among beechwoods, was the home of the Barnsley brothers and Gimson early in the century. Here they added a new wing, designed and built panelled rooms and a chimneypiece and Gimson created a fine plaster ceiling. Later, this house was the home of John Masefield, poet and novelist.

But it is in Sapperton village itself that the evidence of the success of the crafts movement in the lives of the people can best be seen. It makes an intriguing exercise walking round the village trying to detect the identity of the houses built by Gimson and his friends from those erected two centuries or so earlier. Among the former can be seen two houses built by the Barnsley brothers for themselves – Beechanger (Sidney Barnsley, 1903, with its distinctive little dovecote) and Upper Dorvel House, Ernest Barnsley's house of the same date. Ernest Gimson built the Leasowes during the same year. Norman Jewson's skills can be seen in the altered Bachelor's Court, while the village hall of 1912 is also the work of Ernest Barnsley.

St. Kenelm's churchyard contains the graves of Gimson and the Barnsleys, all marked with traditional plain stone slabs bearing brass memorial plates. Inside the church can be seen the ornate monument to Sir Robert Atkyns, Gloucestershire's first historian, who died in 1711, and finely-carved bench ends taken from Sapperton House, demolished in 1730.

Building styles of an entirely different age and purpose can be seen during the short section of the walk along the Severn-Thames canal, from the Daneway Inn to the mouth of the Sapperton tunnel. The inn, formerly known as the Bricklayers' Arms, was built in the 1780s to serve the needs of the men engaged on the construction of the canal tunnel, and later catered for the bargees and 'leggers' who propelled the boats through.

The tunnel entrance (1789) once had an embattled parapet, as can be seen on old photographs. Canal enthusiasts may wish to drive to Coates to see the restored entrance at the other end of the 3,817-yard tunnel.

Route directions

Walk down the lane towards the church. After passing a first footpath on the left, take the second path, which leaves the road just past the old school. This path crosses a field to a handgate and then leads to the churchyard through a lychgate. Leave the churchyard by a stile alongside the main gate. Cross the Manor drive and follow the lane descending to the village. At the lane end, cross the stile and take the footpath (yellow arrow) climbing to a stile at the top of the slope. Leave the field through two gates and aim fo a gap between two houses ahead. The path crosses one fence and passes between two more before turning right to reach a road at a drive entrance.

Climb the stile immediately opposite and cross a large field half-left. Cross the next field, passing an ancient holly tree, to go through a gate in the hedge ahead. Descend towards a house on the bank ahead, crossing half left to a stile in a hedge. Keep a hedge on the left and cross another stile. Cross the next field, passing over a lane and climbing to the left of the house. Aim now for a corner formed by a wall and a hedge. Keep this hedge on the right along the entire length of a large field. Leave the field through a gate and descend into the valley ahead, bearing right along a well-worn path and crossing two stiles before swinging to the left to reach a road opposite Daneway House.

Turn right to the Daneway Inn. From the bridge, follow the footpath signposted Sapperton. The River Frome is on the right and the Thames and Severn Canal on the left. From the tunnel mouth, climb by a ruined cottage above the tunnel and cross a stile. Sapperton lies ahead and is reached along a clear path. Pass a water trough and keep a hedge on the right to reach the churchyard via a kissing gate. The Bell Inn is on the left along the lane climbing from the main churchyard gate.

To continue the walk from the churchyard gate, follow the signposted bridleway by the phone box. Cross a field and go through a handgate. Keep a hedge on the left as far as a handgate on the left. The path now turns left and then right in 20 yards to enter woodland. Leave through a gate and keep straight on, with beeches on the slope to the right. On meeting a curving track climbing the slope, keep left along it through a gate with Pinbury Park visible ahead. Take the track heading to the right of the house, which sweeps to the right to reach a gate. Turn left, passing a pond on the right to meet a drive. Turn left along it. Beyond the house, follow a dipping track towards the woods. This track swings to the right and soon afterwards the path crosses a footbridge and enters the woods through two gates.

There follows a stiff climb through the woods and beyond. Leave the woods through a gateway and keep a low wall on the right. At the top of a sloping field, watch for a stile on the right under a beech tree. This is Gloucester Beeches. Cross the stile and keep a wall on the right to the end of a field. Go through a handgate (Edgeworth can be seen ahead) and keep a fence on the right through another gate. The village is reached by crossing a fence and descending, aiming for the stile by the left-hand cottage, crossed earlier. Retrace steps through the village and back to the start.

Belvedere Mill, Chalford

Walk 16
The Golden Valley — Weavers and a waterway

Theme: The industrial history of the Golden Valley (Valley of the River Frome) and the part played by the Thames & Severn Canal in the changing face of the region.

Start and finish: Layby along the A419 between Chalford church and Chalford Vale.

Getting there: Chalford lies on the A419, 4½ miles SE of Stroud.

Route of walk: Chalford — Brimscombe — Thrupp — Nether Lypiatt — Toadsmoor Valley — Bussage — Chalford Hill — Chalford.

Distance: 8⅓ miles.

Summary of terrain: Flat to begin with (canal towpath). Steep climb through Thrupp to Nether Lypiatt. Steep descent back to Chalford (wet underfoot after rain).

O.S. Sheets: Landranger 163 — Cheltenham & Cirencester area — and Landranger 162 — Gloucester & Forest of Dean (both 1¼ inches to 1 mile).

Starting point grid ref: Sheet 163 — 894026.

Parking: Layby on A419.

Refreshments: Ship Inn, Brimscombe. Ram Inn, Bussage.

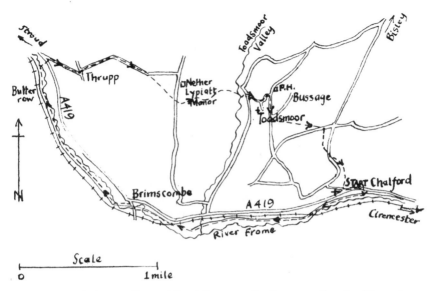

Recommended reading: The Thames & Severn Canal, Humphrey Household, Alan Sutton, 1983.
The Stroudwater and Thames & Severn Canals in Old Photographs. Cuss and Gardiner, Alan Sutton, 1988.

Theme
The valley of the little River Frome between Sapperton and Stroud is often called the Golden Valley — on account, some say, of its glorious autumnal tints. To the poverty-stricken cottage weavers of 200 years ago, however, the gold represented the wealth made by the wealthy millowners from their ill-rewarded labours.

This walk begins at Chalford and follows the towpath of the disused Thames and Severn Canal — not, as do most published walks, eastwards through a pastoral well-wooded landscape towards the tunnel mouth at Daneway and Sapperton — but westwards to the site of the old inland port of Brimscombe and then up the Toadsmoor valley and back down to Chalford along the steep and narrow ways once used by pack-donkeys carrying wool, yarn and finished cloth.

Chalford is a large village, sprawling along the valley and climbing up the hillside on a series of terraces, where former weavers' cottages are linked by the narrow winding roads and paths often too steep for cars. The last of the working woollen mills, Seville's, was demolished in 1952, though cog-wheels from its machinery are still preserved by the canal roundhouse near the start of the walk. Other former mill buildings are passed on the walk and are referred to in the route section. They serve as a reminder of the extensive nature of the woollen industry during its boom years — between 1800 and 1825, almost 200 new mills were erected in the Stroud area. Glimpses can also be had of some of the imposing houses built by the prosperous millowners, perched high above the mills.

Although the 28-mile canal linking the Thames and Severn was opened in 1789, its role in the woollen industry was limited to the transport of coal from the Forest of Dean coalfield, together with associated chemicals and timber. In fact the canal's efficiency was impaired from the start, largely by lack of water but also by constructional defects. The opening of the nearby railway in the 1840s soon brought about keen competition for trade, and despite the spending of considerable sums on restoration work, the waterway closed in 1927 and was abandoned six years later.

The route follows the towpath to Brimscombe, once an important trans-shipment port, where cargoes from the wide Severn trows were transferred to and from the narrow Thames barges. A plaque on the wall of the offices of a new factory marks the place where, until 1962, stood an extensive group of buildings — wharves, warehouses, lengthsmen's cottages, barge-weighing sheds and a salt store, which alone was spared. Nearby, from the 1880's until the Second World War, was a boatyard, at which a range of craft for use in Africa and South America was built.

Brimscombe port is now the site of a modern industrial complex, but such old features as the Ship Inn, with its Severn trow sign, are monuments to its former importance.

The steep climb through Thrupp and over the lower Toadsmoor valley provides a sharp contrast with the bustling Frome valley. Here, streams rush through deeply incised miniature gorges, while up above, open country, once crossed by trains of pack-donkeys, stretches away towards Bisley. Bussage, clinging to the upper slopes, is growing fast but this new development is soon left behind as the route dips along old trackways back down Chalford Hill to the Frome valley.

Route directions
Cross the A419 and follow the signpost indicating the Hyde and Minchinhampton. After seeing the round house, the cog wheels from Saville's Mill and Belvedere Mill, follow the towpath in the direction of Stroud, along the valley of the River Frome.

Beyond Iles Mill the canal is directed along a culvert and the towpath passes under the railway. Eventually the canal bed is almost dry. Modern factories, chiefly producing plastics, line the banks. At Bourne Mills, the towpath passes under the railway and follows the river towards

Brimscombe, where the old port is now an industrial estate. The route now climbs over a bridge above a well-preserved mill. Just beyond the Ship Inn turn left along a private road. The route keeps along the factory wall with the canal on the left. At a second red-bricked bridge, the path dips to follow the canal once more.

The route leaves the canal towpath at a stile on the right just before a red-bricked bridge, over which a path leads up to the hamlet of Butter Row, perched on the hillside on the left. Instead of going in that direction, aim for the A419, keeping a wire fence on the left. Cross a low bridge and a stile to reach the road. Cross and turn left. In a short distance turn sharp right up Thrupp Lane. At the top turn left along Claypits Lane and right by Thrupp Farm. Climb the steep narrow lane, ignoring side-turns.

Eventually, at the top of the slope, and with Nether Lypiatt Manor visible ahead, take the footpath on the right signposted Mackhouse Wood. The path crosses a field diagonally to a stile and then follows the side of a wood on the left to a lane. Cross the lane, following the signpost Mackhouse and Toadsmoor. Bear left, passing an 'Unsuitable for Motors' sign. At the bottom of the lane, bear right at a fork and keep on to reach a road. Cross and climb Bussage Hill. Bear left at a fork and continue climbing to reach the Ram Inn.

Turn right and keep straight on, passing Bussage village hall and a phone box on the right. Where a footpath crosses the road, turn left, and after passing through a modern housing estate, enter a wood. Beyond, cross a road and follow a footpath between stone walls to the left of a cemetery. On reaching a road, turn right (no pavement), and in a short distance, turn left at an 'Unsuitable for Motors' sign, for a steep descent to reach the A419 by Chalford church. The layby is on the left.

Bibury

Walk 17
The Coln Valley — Arthur Gibbs country

Theme: The valley of the River Coln, part of the Cotswolds rich in literary associations, and especially those relating to J. Arthur Gibbs, squire of Ablington, near Bibury, author of 'A Cotswold Village'.

Start and finish: Calcot.

Getting there: Calcot lies 1½ miles east of the A429, 3 miles north-west of Bibury.

Route of walk: Calcot — Coln Rogers — Winson — Ablington Downs — Saltway Barns — Bibury — Arlington — Ablington — Calcot.

Distance: 9 miles.

Summary of terrain: Undulating. A few stiffish ascents (on Cotswold standards).

O.S. Sheet: Landranger 163 — Cheltenham and Cirencester area (1¼ inches to 1 mile).

Starting point grid ref: 001101.

Parking: Limited parking on grass verge above Calcot.

Refreshments: Catherine Wheel Inn, Arlington.

Recommended reading: A Cotswold Village. J. Arthur Gibbs, Murray, 1898. (reprinted many times since).

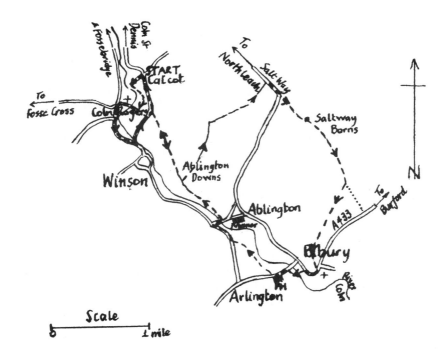

Through the Valley. Robert Henriques, Collins, 1950
Recommended to visit: Arlington Mill museum, Bibury.

Theme

The Coln Valley — and more especially the stretch of water at Bibury — has been a tourist attraction for close on a century. It was in 1890 that William Morris, the poet and craftsman, journeyed over from his home at Kelmscott and proclaimed Bibury as the most beautiful village in England. Since then, a steady stream of tourists — and writers too — have heaped further praise upon this lovely place, with its pure waters, tame ducks, trout farm, cottages, museum and so on.

But there is more to the Coln Valley than Bibury, as those who have taken the trouble to walk its footpaths will readily agree. As also would have J. Arthur Gibbs, the young squire of nearby Ablington, whose book, 'A Cotswold Village', published shortly before his tragically early death in 1898, reveals in generous measure. Gibbs's book is sub-titled 'Country Life and Pursuits in Gloucestershire', and as could be expected, contains a good deal of writing on field sports — hunting, shooting and fishing. But the author was also a good naturalist and had a eye for scenic beauty and a fluent pen with which to describe it:

'Never shall I forget seeing this old place (Bibury) from the hill above during one September sunset. There was a marvellous glow suffused over the western sky, infinitely beautiful while it lasted; and immediately below a silvery mist had risen from the surface of the broad trout stream, and was hanging over the old Norman tower of the church. Amid the rush of the waterfall could be heard the distant voices of children in the village street.'

Gibbs's old home, Ablington Manor, built in 1590, can be glimpsed over its screening wall during the walk, as can the splendid barns he knew well close by. Farming methods have changed since 'A Cotswold Village' first appeared but the sweeping contours of Ablington Downs remain much as they did in Gibbs's day. The wildlife too, though reduced in numbers, is still varied, especially the birds. Grey wagtails and dippers can be spotted along the waterside, together with herons, dabchicks and mallard.

Among the flowers, such water-loving species as lady's smock, kingcup, water mint and monkey flower are abundant, together with purple loosestrife, great willow herb, comfrey and butterdock. Colourful dragonflies and their smaller relatives, the damsel flies, are a feature of the waterside during the summer months, and mayflies — beloved of Gibbs and other trout fishermen — live out their brief lives in abundance in May.

The village of Winson, approached early in the walk, was the home of the novelist Robert Henriques, several of whose works were set in the local countryside. 'Through the Valley', with its strong story line and close associations with the Coln Valley, is perhaps the best, but 'A Stranger Here' and 'The Journey Home' also provide an absorbing read.

The Coln can be traced through Coln St. Aldwyns and Fairford down to its meeting place with the Thames at Lechlade. Northwards, the following of its course from its source on the flanks of Cleeve Hill, through Brockhampton, Sevenhampton, Withington and Chedworth, makes another rewarding experience.

Route directions

Walk down the hill through Calcot. At the foot of the slope, the road becomes a footpath, leading to a bridge over the River Coln. Instead of crossing, follow another footpath to the left over a stile. Keep along the river bank and enter a wood through a handgate. After leaving the wood, cross a footbridge by a garden and keep on to reach Coln Rogers.

Beyond the church, turn left at the T-junction for Winson. Before reaching the village, where the road swings right to cross a bridge, turn left up the lane signposted Calcot and Northleach. At the top of the slope, as the road bends to the left, turn sharp right along a bridleway. Ignore a track on the left leading to a barn. Go through a gate and keep straight on, with a wall on the left. Dip through a gateway and descend to a valley bottom.

Just after passing two gates on the right, and before reaching another, straight ahead, turn left along the valley, keeping damp ground on the left. The route eventually traces a meandering grassy track along a dry valley through Ablington Downs. Keep on through a gate with woodland on the slope to the right, and two more on either side of barns on the left. Bear right and climb, passing a wood on the left, until the track swings and climbs to the right. At this point, leave it and go through the left of two gates, following a track with a wall on the right to reach a road.

Turn right along the Salt Way. After passing cottages, the road bends to the right. Keep straight on here to reach Saltway Barns. Just beyond the farm buildings, turn left through a metal gate and then immediately right along another track, keeping a hedge on the right. Pass a wood on the right and after the track bends right and is joined by another from the left, turn right through a metal gate. Head for a barn, keeping a wall on the right. After passing the barn and a farm lane on the left, keep a wall on the left along a lane (metalled at first), before continuing down a drive to meet a road. Turn right into Bibury.

Approaching Bibury bridge, turn left over a footbridge to see Arlington Row, after which a metalled path to the right follows the mill stream to Arlington Mill (now a museum). The route continues by climbing left up the road to Arlington. (The Catherine Wheel Inn is on the left.) Opposite the phone box, turn right along a lane indicated as a 'No through road'. At a fork, bear left and follow the public footpath sign along a drive. Keep straight on, crossing stiles, as far as a cottage, which is passed on the left through a gate to reach a road. Turn right and right again for Ablington. Arthur Gibbs's home, the Manor, is on the right and can be glimpsed over a high wall.

To continue the walk, retrace as far as Elm Tree Cottage and climb the lane, with the mill stream on the left. This lane eventually links up with the outward route at the point where the section along the valley through Ablington Downs commenced. Retrace to the end of the bridleway and then keep straight on along the lane for Calcot and the starting point.

Little Barrington

Walk 18

Cotswold Stone — Burford and the Barringtons

Theme: An exploration of the lower Windrush valley, from which some of the finest Cotswold stone has been quarried, and which in Burford and its neighbouring borderland villages, possesses some of the finest architecture in the region.

Start and finish: The riverside car park near Burford church.

Getting there: Burford lies off the A40, between Cheltenham and Oxford.

Route of walk: Burford — Taynton — Miletree Clump — Great Rissington — Great Barrington — Little Barrington — Upton — Burford.

Distance: 11½ miles.

Summary of terrain: A mix of footpath and minor-road walking with a few gentle gradients.

O.S. Sheet: Landranger 163 — Cheltenham & Cirencester area (1¼ inches to 1 mile).

Starting point grid ref: 255123.

Parking: See start.

Refreshments: Lamb Inn, Great Rissington. Fox Inn, Barrington. Choice of inns and cafés in Burford.

Recommended reading: Burford Past & Present, Mr. Sturge Gretton, Faber, 1945.

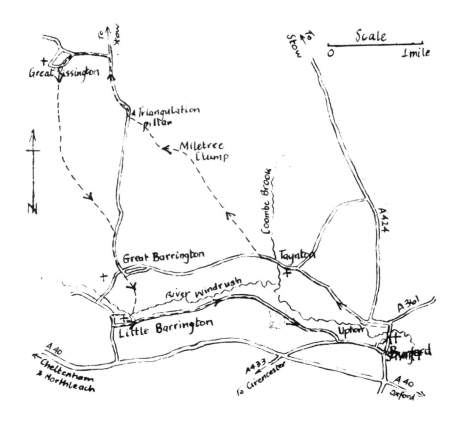

The Book of Burford, R. & J. Moody, Barracuda, 1984.
Cotswold Stone, Freda Derrick, Chapman & Hall, 1948.

Theme

Although this walk starts outside Gloucestershire — Burford and its near neighbour, Taynton, being just in Oxfordshire — the other villages on the route — Great Rissington and the Barringtons — lie in Gloucestershire.

The little town of Burford, often referred to as the 'Gateway to the Cotswolds', is a gem among towns. The locally-quarried honey-coloured limestone has been fashioned so skilfully over the centuries that there is scarcely a jarring note — the church, the Tolsey, the inns, houses, schools — all bear witness to the grace and durability of this unique building material. The Norman church of St. John the Baptist, filled to the doors with treasures and possessing a churchyard crammed with superb bale top tombs, reminds us that the wool trade brought prosperity to

85

Burford, and a walk up High Street confirms this. But it is only by seeking out the side streets and odd little corners, and in so doing shaking off the constant intrusion of traffic, that the real atmosphere of the place can be enjoyed.

The Taynton quarries, reached by a side road on the right of the route through the village, have long been silent, but their reputation remains. The list of famous buildings built from Taynton stone could hardly be more impressive — Merton College, Oxford; Eton College; St. George's Chapel, Windsor; Blenheim Palace — yet we need to go much further back into history, possibly as far as Roman times, to arrive at some idea of their antiquity. The village itself, though attractive and unspoilt, lacks any notable buildings.

Beyond Taynton, the route climbs through open arable country, crossing into Gloucestershire at Miletree Clump before striking the road to Great Rissington, southernmost of three spring-line villages overlooking the Vale of Bourton. Like its neighbours this is a prosperous enough place now, its well-cared-for stone buildings harmonising with the surrounding landscape, but it has known hard times. One writer, visiting here during the agricultural depression just before the First World War, described its derelict state: 'The tragedy of rural England stood unmasked without even the glamour of the picturesque, as though the army of some conquering foreigner had invaded the Cotswold Hills and riddled the cottages with holes.' Now, in happy contrast, school, inn, cottages and church all thrive, indicating that village life is in a healthy state.

The Barringtons provide something of a contrast. Workaday Great Barrington until quite recently experienced a decline similar to that suffered by Great Rissington earlier in the century. Now, however, an extensive restoration scheme is nearing completion and once the new stone has mellowed the village will take its rightful place among its well-groomed neighbours.

Little Barrington, on the other hand, has retained its charm if not its homespun Cotswold character. Its old water mill long since ceased to grind corn and we can easily miss noticing the remains of the wharf at the end of the causeway from Great Barrington, where the Strong family loaded their stone onto boats for the journey down to the Thames for Oxford and London.

The switchback lane from Little Barrington back through Upton to Burford provides delightful views of the River Windrush. At the junction of this lane with the main road into the town, a glimpse can be had to the right of Kitt's Quarry, the house built for himself by Christopher Kempster, friend of Christopher Wren, and master mason of Burford.

Route directions

From the car park, bear right, passing the almshouses and church on the right to reach High Street. Turn right and cross the bridge over the River Windrush. By the junction of the A361 (Chipping Norton) and A424 (Stow) roads, cross a stile in the wall on the left to follow the footpath parallel to the A424 over water meadows. Ignore a left fork leading to a bridge. Instead, keep straight on until a slab-stile is reached alongside the lane leading to Taynton. Follow this lane to the village.

Beyond Taynton, as the road levels out, follow the signposted public bridleway on the right. After a steady climb, pass farm buildings on the right to reach a wood (Miletree Clump). The bridleway passes between the wood and a hedge. Beyond the wood, keep a hedge on the left and aim for a clump of trees ahead. Pass the clump and cross a field towards a white triangulation pillar by the roadside. Turn right along the road as far as the turn on the left to Great Rissington.

Descend to the village. The Lamb Inn is just beyond the little green at the foot of the slope. The route continues along the village street on the left. Leave the street along a lane on the left just before reaching the postbox on the right. This lane is a bridleway, leading to Great Barrington. Keep straight on along it, ignoring side-turns. Eventually, after keeping a hedge on the left, the route descends to cross a cart bridge to the left of a hedge, after which it climbs along a winding track to Great Barrington.

Turn right into the village, passing Barrington Park on the right. The route leaves the village along a narrow lane marked by derestriction signs near the war memorial. When this lane veers to the left, keep straight on down a track to Barrington Mill (now a private house). After crossing the mill stream, walk along the causeway to cross the Windrush at Little Barrington. To see this village, turn right along the narrow footpath which leads to the centre of the village. (Those wishing to omit the village can turn left and climb past cottages to the lane leading back to Burford.)

From Little Barrington village, take the minor road on the left, passing the church on the left and meandering pleasantly along the Windrush valley past Papermill Cottages, through Upton, to reach a junction with another road opposite a cemetery. (Kitts Quarry is to the right of the cemetery.)

Turn left along the road back to Burford, passing the hospital and entering the town along Sheep Street. The car park is down the hill on the right.

Lower Slaughter

Walk 19
The Vale of Bourton — birdlife by lake and river

Theme: The wildlife — especially birds — along the Eye, Dikler and Windrush valleys.

Start and finish: The bridge over the Eye at the southern end of Lower Slaughter.

Getting there: Lower Slaughter lies just off the A429, 2 miles north of Bourton-on-the-Water.

Route of walk: Lower Slaughter — Fosse Way (A429) — Rissington Mill — Leasow Lane — Nethercote — Bourton-on-the-Water — Lower Slaughter.

Distance: 7½ miles.

Summary of terrain: A few gentle climbs and a short stretch of road walking (Leasow Lane). Wet patches around lakes in winter.

O.S. Sheet: Landranger 163 — Cheltenham & Cirencester area (1¼ inches to 1 mile).

Starting point grid ref: 165225.

Parking: Limited parking in Lower Slaughter.

Refreshments: Plenty of choice (cafes and inns) in Bourton.

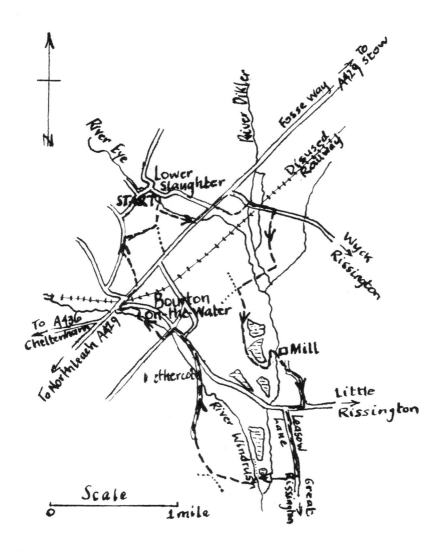

Recommended reading: Birds of Gloucestershire. C.M. Swaine, Alan
    Sutton, 1982.
Recommended to visit: Birdland, Bourton-on-the-Water.

Theme
    The Vale of Bourton is the name given to the area around the village
of Bourton-on-the-Water, which includes the valley of the River
Windrush and those of its two tributary rivers, the Eye and the Dikler.

In addition to these attractions however, the bird watching scope of this walk is greatly extended by the presence nearby of a chain of worked-out gravel pits, which, since the 1970s, have been landscaped and stocked with fish. With the passing of years these 'lakes' have blended into the scenery to such an extent that tourists have been heard to remark that Bourton owes the 'on-the-Water' part of its name to their presence.

Wetland bird populations vary according to the time of the year. During spring and summer, such resident species as great-crested grebe, little grebe, coot, moorhen, mallard and tufted duck all breed with varying success around the lakes. Larger resident species − mute swan, Canada goose and heron − can often be seen feeding, while black-headed gulls, kingfishers and pied wagtails frequently occur. Overhead, the sky is busy with clouds of swallows, martins and swifts, hawking for insects which are alway plentiful above the water.

Between October and March, the lakes provide congenial winter quarters for large numbers of waterfowl, chiefly ducks, of which pochard and wigeon are usually the most abundant. Great rafts of these ducks sit on the water, their numbers augmented from time to time by other ducks, including pintail and shoveler. Among the less-common species of water birds recorded on the lakes over the years are cormorant, goosander, goldeneye, shelduck and barnacle goose.

Away from the lakes, the riverside walk brings its own bird-watching opportunities. It is always worth looking closely at the waterwheel at Lower Slaughter mill, for this spot is often favoured by a beautiful sulphur-breasted grey wagtail. Throughout the walk, clear, fast-flowing rivers attract the dipper − a stumpy-looking brownish bird of starling size, but with a prominent white bib, which stands out when the bird alights on a boulder in mid-water and stands motionless apart from the odd curtseying movement for which it is noted. Like kingfishers, dippers fly rapidly close the water, though they lack the colourful appearance of that familiar if seldom-seen waterside bird.

Riverside bird life is not confined solely to the water. For much of the walk, the banks are lined with trees, of which alders and willows are the dominant species. The rounded little cones of the alder attract several species of finches, inluding siskins and redpolls, which rival the tit tribe in their antics. The willows, too, appeal to certain birds, among which are the little owl, which often nests in the holes in old willows, and tits and treecreepers, which find the willows' deeply grooved barn a profitable source of insect food.

While for those walkers who wish to extend their birdwatching to include the collection of exotic species established at Bourton by the late

Len Hill, 'Birdland's' celebrated grounds are close at hand on the closing stages of the walk.

Route directions

After seeing the village, leave the church on the left and take the riverside path beyond the road bridge. At a stile, turn left along a signposted footpath, with the River Eye on the left. Cross 3 stiles to reach the A429 (Fosse Way). Cross and turn left along the pavement as far as a gate by a cottage, opposite the turn to the Slaughters.

Follow the track into a narrow field. Where the field widens, keep on along the raised track diagonally across the field. Go over a bridge and through a gate to reach a road. Turn right. Cross a railway bridge and turn right through the first of two gates sharing a wide entrance. Keep a hedge on the left as far as another gate. Go through and keep the hedge on the right as far as the River Dikler, which is crossed by a cart bridge. Now follow the Oxfordshire Way signs over 3 bridges to the top right-hand corner of a field. Pass through a kissing gate and leave the Oxfordshire Way by turning left along a grassy lane.

Keep straight on as far as a power pole. From here, bear left through a gateway and then right by the field edge to cross a stream and a stile to reach a lake. Keep the lake on the left and cross a stile to reach a path between two more lakes. When this path forks, turn left along a narrow path with lakes on either side. Eventually, the path bends to the left to cross a footbridge and pass through a gate in the hedge on the right.

Cross a meadow to another stile and veer right along the river bank (the Dikler). Cross two footbridges and follow the path round Rissington Mill to reach a drive. Turn right along it, keeping on to reach the Bourton-Rissington road at the foot of a hill. Turn right along a pavement as far as Leasow Lane, leading to Great Rissington. Cross the road to follow the lane.

In about half a mile, and about 100 yards beyond a barn on the right, turn right through a gate along a signposted footpath. Keep a hedge on the right through two fields and cross a gated bridge over the Dikler. The riverside path soon swings to the right and passes through a handgate. Keep a small lake on the right as far as the River Windrush. Turn left along it and cross two footbridges and a stile. Turn right, keeping a stream on the right. Cross two stiles to reach a lane coming in from the left. Keep straight on along it, crossing a stile to reach a minor road. Turn right along it and follow it all the way to its junction with the Rissington Road at Nethercote, on the outskirts of Bourton. Turn left into the village.

Continuing the walk from Bourton, cross the Windrush by the bridge near the war memorial. Where the road forks, take the signposted footpath between houses on the right. This path follows the river bank and reaches the road at Mill House. Turn left along the pavement to Bourton Bridge and the A429 (Fosse Way).

Do not cross the busy road here. Instead, follow the pavement towards Stow. Not far beyond the left turn signposted to Naunton, cross and follow a signposted footpath over a stile in the hedge. Cross two more stiles and climb a field. In the next field, reached over two more stiles, cross diagonally to the right and go through a gate to reach the road. Turn right along it as far as a handgate on the right. Go through this and descend a field, keeping a hedge on the left, to meet another footpath near a gate. Pass through this gate and keep straight on for Lower Slaughter, passing the stile crossed at the start of walk and retracing steps back to the starting point.

Condicote Lane (Ryknild Street)

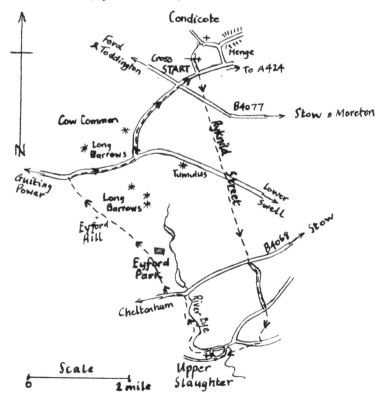

Walk 20

In the steps of the Romans — Ryknild Street and Condicote

Theme: Condicote Lane — the southernmost section of Rynkild Street, a Roman road which played an important part in the colonisation of the north Cotswolds and in the administration of Britain generally in Roman times.

Start and finish: Condicote village green.

Getting there: Condicote lies a mile north of the B4007 and four miles NW of Stow-on-the-Wold.

Route of walk: Condicote — Condicote Lane — Upper Slaughter — Eyford Park — Eyford Hill — Condicote.

Distance: 8½ miles.

Summary of terrain: Generally easy walking along footpaths and minor roads, with only a few uphill stretches. Beware of electric fences near Upper Slaughter (notes in route description).

O.S. Sheet: Landranger 163 — Cheltenham & Cirencester area (1¼ inches to 1 mile).

Starting point grid ref: 152283.

Parking: By village green.

Refreshments: No inn on route. Good choice at Stow and Bourton.

Recommended reading: Roman Gloucestershire, A. McWhirr, Alan Sutton, 1981.

Theme

Rynkild Street is the only Roman road with one of its extremities lying within Gloucestershire. It is generally agreed that it is prehistoric in origin, at least for some of its length; what is certain is that it was one of the main Roman roads of the Midlands, and extended from the Fosse Way at Bourton-on-the-Water in a north-westerly direction, leaving the county near Weston-sub-Edge, and proceeding through Bidford-on-Avon, Alcester and Studley. Beyond Birmingham, the road crossed Watling Street at Wall, near Lichfield, before turning north-east for Burton-on-Trent and Derby and entering Yorkshire to reach Templeborough, near Rotherham.

Like other Roman roads, Ryknild Street has only partially survived to the present day. Considerable stretches now carry modern roads — between Bidford and Wixford it is known as the B4085; the section near Studley is now the A435, and that part between Burton and Derby is the bustling A38. By contrast, some lengthy stretches of Ryknild Street have disappeared completely, with scarcely a trace of the agger (embankment) now visible.

For the walker, the most appealing sections of Roman roads are those which have survived as green lanes and this walk is routed to include one of the best stretches — that from the village of Condicote south-eastwards towards Upper Slaughter and the Fosse Way. Unfortunately, the final section that once linked the two roads has been lost — a pity, as Bourton was an important staging post in Roman times and extensive remains have been excavated in the vicinity.

Even without being able to make this link, however, the two-mile walk along this southern limit of Ryknild Street is a memorable experience. Condicote, the starting point, is a lonely upland village grouped around a walled green with an ancient cross and a Norman church, as well as the remains of a henge (prehistoric earthwork) on its eastern extremity. It has given its name to this green-lane section of the Roman road, as the Ordnance Survey map reveals — a name originating no doubt from the times when drovers made use of this section on their cross-country journeys.

Further north, between Saintbury and Weston-sub-Edge (see Walk 15), Ryknild Street was known as Buggildeway, or Buggeldway — said to have been variations of the word buculus, meaning a bullock — another connection with the cattle drovers of medieval times. Later, the name evolved to become Buckle Street — still used on maps showing the stretch of the Roman road from Saintbury northward beyond Honeybourne, towards Bidford-on-Avon.

Evidence of significant pre-Roman settlement in the vicinity of Ryknild Street has been established north of Eyford Park and at Cow Common, 1½ miles south-west of Condicote, and passed during the return stretch of the walk. A Bronze Age cemetery consisting of ten round barrows and one of the long type were excavated here during the last century. Both burials and cremations were found, together with neolithic pottery, spoons and a razor.

Route directions

Leave Condicote by the lane nearest the cross. Pass College Farm and keep on to a T-junction, signposted Stow and Tewkesbury. Cross this road and keep on along the track marked 'Unsuitable for motors'. This is Ryknild Street, known locally as Condicote Lane. Cross the B4077. Soon, Stow church can be seen on the left and the TV mast on Icomb Hill slightly to the right.

Beyond the B4068 the route is metalled as far as a T-junction. Yellow arrows now indicate the route. Keep straight on through a gate and in 70 yards, bear right through a gateway, keeping a wall on the right, towards an avenue of trees. Cross a drive by two stiles into woodland and follow the meandering path down to a gate. Bear left along a fence down a field towards a road, which is reached over two stiles.

Turn right along the road and in a short distance, watch for a stile on the left opposite a gate. Cross and follow the path, which keeps the hedge on the right before passing through a gateway. Follow the yellow signs over two fields and down a slope to cross a stream and climb to a road. Turn left into Upper Slaughter. (If this stile is blocked by an electric fence, reach the path over the next gate.)

From the village centre, follow the road signposted 'Unsuitable for motors'. Dip past a 'No through road' sign on the left to follow a lane with the River Eye on the right. Go through a handgate and climb a grassy track ahead. After passing through another handgate, the path dips to enter a wood through a gate by a cottage. The route now follows a riverside track. Turn left at a fork to reach the B4068. Turn left (no pavement) and keep on as far as a signposted bridleway on the right, just before a row of cottages.

To begin with, this stretch of the route follows a metalled drive. Pass the entrance to Eyford Park. Beyond, the drive passes farm buildings, after which it becomes a track. Keep straight on, passing more farm buildings (Eyford Hill), to reach a road. Turn right, and at the foot of a hill, left for Condicote. After crossing the B4077 and turning left at the next junction, the return to Condicote is made by retracing steps along the first metalled stretch of Ryknild Street walked earlier.

Evenlode between Kingham and Bledington

Walk 21

The Evenlode Valley – 'All the birds of Oxfordshire and Gloucestershire'.

Theme: Bird life along the Evenlode Valley – and its associations with the poet Edward Thomas and the ornithologist William Warde Fowler.

Start and finish: The bus shelter, Adlestrop.

Getting there: Adlestrop lies a mile north of the A436 and 4 miles east of Stow-on-the-Wold.

Route of walk: Adlestrop (village) – Daylesford – Kingham – Bledington – Oddington (St Nicholas' church) – Oddington – Adlestrop (railway bridge) – Adlestrop.

Distance: 8½ miles.

Summary of terrain: No gradients worth speaking of. Bridleway from Bledington to Oddington old church *very* mudddy.

O.S. Sheet: Landranger 163 – Cheltenham and Cirencester area (1½ inches to 1 mile).

Starting point grid ref: 242272.

Refreshments: Plough Inn, Kingham. King's Arms, Bledington.

Recommended reading: Collected Poems. Edward Thomas, Faber, 1974

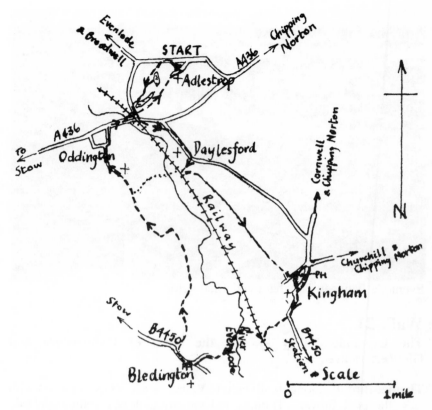

Warde Fowler's Countryside. Gordon Ottewell (Ed), Severn House, 1985.

Theme

It is a rare event to find a poet honoured by a village in which he never set foot. Edward Thomas's link with Adlestrop is based solely on a short poem he wrote after the train on which he was travelling stopped at the little station one afternoon in late June. It was the time of the First World War, in which Thomas, like thousands of his contemporaries, was to die in the wastes of Flanders. But the poem struck a responsive chord and when the station closed in 1964, its nameboard was re-erected in the village and 'Adlestrop' — the poem — was displayed alongside in the bus shelter.

Although he came to poetry late in his comparatively short life, Edward Thomas's love of nature was clearly evident in his many prose works. He took as his model the Victorian country writer Richard Jefferies, of whom he was a biographer, and his essays and travel guides are rich in descriptive passages of great sensitivity. Together with wild flowers, birds and a special place in his affections and his poetry contains many finely-observed references:

'A wagtail flickered bright over the mill-pond's gloom.'
'The swift with wings and tail as sharp and narrow
As if the bow had flown off with the arrow.'
'It is a kind of spring: the chaffinch tries his song.'
'And sedge-warblers clinging so light
To willow twigs, sang longer than the lark.'

During his time at Oxford, Thomas had admired the nature writings of William Warde Fowler, a classical don who lived in the Oxfordshire village of Kingham, just over the border from Adlestrop. Fowler was something of a pioneer in the field of ornithology, being a student of living birds, rather than relying on the collecting of specimens, and his books − long out of print − did a valuable service to the countryside, and to bird-protection in particular, by encouraging his readers to watch, rather than shoot and rob birds.

Fowler had a distinct preference for smaller birds, especially wagtails, redstarts and warblers. About the former, he wrote:
'It is impossible ever to weary of wagtails. We are never altogether without them, yet whenever they present themselves to us we are constrained to give them our attention. Some birds you can glance at as you walk and talk but no sooner does a wagtail alight in front of you than he compels you to pause and look at him carefully.'

Fowler's speciality was the rare marsh warbler, which he studied for many years in an osier bed near the railway, passed on the walk. This bird no longer haunts the Evenlode valley, but wagtails − both pied and grey − are frequently encountered, as are kingfishers, herons and mute swans. Lapwings can be seen in large flocks and the hedgerow species − chaffinch, greenfinch, yellowhammer, song thrush and blackbird − are joined during the spring and summer months by whitethroats, blackcaps, willow warblers and spotted flycatchers.

Oddington Ashes, a large tract of woodland passed through during the later stages of walk, offers suitable habitat for woodpeckers, treecreepers, tits and nuthatches, while for those content to gaze in a leisurely fashion at tame ducks, Bledington village green boasts some of the most placid imaginable − complete with their own road-sign warning to reduce speed!

Route directions

From the bus shelter, walk down the road in the direction of Stow. Just beyond a barn on the left, follow a footpath sign over a stile. Pass a pond on the left and cross a field diagonally to a bridge over a ditch.

Keep the stream and hedge on the left round a large field to reach a road. Turn left, passing a lake on the left, to reach the A436. Cross to pass through a handgate. Cross a field diagonally to reach a road over a gate. Turn right into Daylesford. After passing the church on the right, take a footpath, also on the right, signposted Oddington. Just before reaching a bridge over the railway, turn left and cross the field just passed through to reach a metal gate, leading to a bridleway. Keep hedges on the left, passing a small wood on the right and a large barn on the left and carry straight on to Kingham.

On entering the village, turn left. Those wishing to see the greater part of the village and/or visit the Plough Inn should keep straight on up West Street and turn right at the village green. Otherwise, turn right and follow the winding lane past houses to reach Church Street. Turn right here for the church. Warde Fowler's grave is on the left just before the porch.

Just beyond the churchyard wall, turn right along a metalled footpath and right again as far as New Road. At this point, follow the signposted footpath between houses to cross the railway. Yellow arrows denote the route. The old osier bed in which Warde Fowler observed the rare marsh warbler is on the left between the railway and the bridge over the River Evenlode. From the bridge, keep a hedge on the right and climb the old railway embankment. Go over a stile on the opposite side and cross a meadow. Go over a footbridge and bear right when the path forks, to a stile at the right-hand corner of the field. Follow the twisting lane into Bledington.

Cross the bridge in front of the Kings Arms Inn, following the Stow road as far as a bridleway sign just past the last house on the right. This bridleway crosses an old railway and later bears to the right at a fork. After meandering through woodland, a short break in the trees is reached. Instead of continuing straight on through a gate into the next wood, turn left, keeping the wood on the right. Soon, the track bends to the right, still keeping close to the woodland edge. Follow it straight on, ignoring side-turns. Eventually, it becomes wider and reaches the old church of St. Nicholas at Oddington.

Beyond the church, keep on up the lane to the village. Turn right and follow the street to its meeting with the A436. Turn right to cross Adlestrop railway bridge. (The site of the station can be seen over the parapet on the left.) After turning left along the Adlestrop road, climb a stile on the right in 20 yards. Cross a field towards a cricket pavilion. Keep to the right-hand edge of the pitch and go through a gate (marked with a blue arrow). Climb the track to Adlestrop, passing the church on the right. Bear left in the village to reach the starting point.

Site of Lower Ditchford

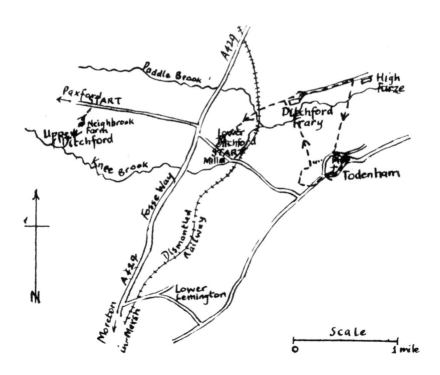

Walk 22

Lost villages — The Ditchfords

Theme: Lost villages. The sites of former settlements long since abandoned.

Start and finish: Route 1 — Ditchford Mill
Route 2 — Top of lane to Neighbrook.

Getting there: Route 1 — Ditchford Mill lies three quarters of a mile east of the A429, three miles NE of Moreton-in-Marsh.
Route 2 — Neighbrook lies west of the A429, three miles north of Morton-in-Marsh.

Route of walk: Route 1 — Ditchford Mill — Lower Ditchford — Ditchford Frary — High Furze — Todenham — Ditchford Frary — Ditchford Mill.
Route 2 — Neighbrook Farm — Neighbrook — Upper Ditchford — (retrace steps).

Distances: Route 1 — Five miles.
Route 2 — One mile.

Summary of terrain: Gently undulating. Stiles frequently damaged or missing. Paths not always obvious.

O.S. Sheet: Landranger 151 — Stratford-on-Avon (1¼ inches to 1 mile).

Starting point grid refs: Route 1 — 226365.
Route 2 — 204373.

Parking: Route 1 — On verge near Ditchford Mill.
Route 2 — On verge near lane down to Neighbrook.

Refreshments: Farriers Arms, Todenham.

Recommended reading: The Lost Villages of England, M. W. Beresford, Lutterworth, 1954. (Reprinted: Alan Sutton, 1985.)
Deserted Villages, T. Rowley and J. Wood, Shire Publications, 1982.

Theme

A glance at a map of the north Cotswolds reveals several sites of abandoned villages. Well-known examples are Upton, near Blockley, Lemington, near Moreton-in-Marsh, and a cluster of three villages on either side of the Fosse Way roughly between Moreton and Shipston-on-Stour, referred to collectively as the Ditchfords.

The name Ditchford occurs frequently in this Gloucestershire-Warwickshire border country. In addition to the abandoned village sites of Upper Ditchford, Lower Ditchford and Ditchford Frary, large-scale maps record a number of farms, woods and other features, among which are Ditchford Farm, Middle Ditchford, Ditchford Hill, Ditchford-on-

Fosse, Ditchford Gorse, Ditchford Cottages and Ditchford Mill — from which the first of the two routes begins.

So many times — yet not a single village now exists by the name of Ditchford. What happened to cause these villages to disappear? Very little has been written about the fate of the Ditchfords but all the evidence points to the creation of extensive sheep-walks as the reason for their decline. According to the writings of John Rouse, a Warwickshire priest and antiquary, dated 1491, the Ditchfords had become ruinous during his lifetime, as had no less than 58 villages in Warwickshire alone.

So although the ravages of plague might seem a more dramatic reason for the abandonment of the Ditchfords, this is hardly likely to be the explanation. However, this is not to say that the hardship borne by the villagers was not great. The menfolk — ploughman, carters and labourers — were deprived of their livelihood and had to move in search of work, taking their families with them and leaving only a few shepherds to occupy the empty villages. In his 'Utopia', Sir Thomas More denounced the all-consuming sheep: 'They destroy and devour whole fields. . .and leave no ground for tillage. They enclose all pastures, they throw down houses, they pluck down towns, and leave nothing standing.'

What remains today are a series of banked and ditched enclosures showing where these villages once stood. At Lower Ditchford, the house-platforms can still be seen, together with what is believed to be the site of a moated manor house. At Ditchford Frary, over the county boundary in Warwickshire, the remains of more recent buildings, including a water mill, still stand, not far from the farmhouse that is the only surviving building to perpetuate the name of the lost village.

Upper Ditchford is more difficult to explore. The village earthworks lie on a south-west facing slope near Neighbrook House and farm. Here again, banked and ditched enclosures can be seen, together with house platforms. To the east lie four large terraces, possibly the site of other buildings. The footpath on this side of the site has been erased and the bridge over the Knee Brook to Aston Magna has gone, which entails retracing steps.

The ford to the left of the footbridge over the Knee Brook between Ditchford Frary and Todenham probably dates back to medieval times, when the old lane was the main route linking the two villages. The hedges, rich in tree and shrub species, and the clearly-indicated ridge-and-furrow of the old ploughland, are further signs of early farming activity.

Route directions Route 1
From Ditchford Mill, walk back along the lane towards the A429. In a short distance, turn right along a rough track. The site of Lower

Ditchford is in the field on the right. Cross the remains of an old railway and pass an ornamental lake on the left. The site of Ditchford Frary is on the right, just before the farm by the side of the track. Beyond the farm, the route lies along a surfaced road. Just before reaching the next farm, High Furze, turn right through a gate. Head towards Todenham church spire, visible through the trees. Bear right at a fork in the track to cross a bridge over the Knee Brook. Follow the grassy track straight ahead to a gate. Beyond, climb an old lane up to Todenham. At the top is a gateway to the manor. For the Farriers Arms and the village, turn left along a lane and keep on to meet a road. Turn right into Todenham.

Beyond the church and village hall, turn right along a signposted footpath. Go through a gate and keep first a brick wall, then a hedge, on the right to the gate at the end of the field. Pass through this gate and immediately turn right through another gate to follow a track between fields. At the end of the track, cross a stile alongside a gate and keep a hedge on the right over a wide field with a farm ahead. About half-way across this field, watch for a metal gate in the hedge. At this point, turn at right angles to the left and cross the ridge and furrow to pass through a metal gate near a corner formed by two hedges. Keep a hedge on the right over another field.

Ditchford Frary farm can now be seen ahead. Aim slightly to the left of the buildings, crossing a fence to descend to the right of a ruined building to reach the remains of an old water mill. Cross the gated bridge and another, smaller bridge in the next field, and make for a gate in the hedge straight ahead. Climb the stile alongside the gate to reach the lane walked earlier. Turn left and then retrace the short distance back to the start.

Route directions Route 2

Walk down the lane, passing Neighbrook Farm on the left. Just beyond the 'Free range children and other animals' sign, cross a stile on the right. The footpath skirts the grounds of Neighbrook House and reaches the drive and the bridge over the Knee Brook. The mounds of Upper Ditchford abandoned village are visible nearby. Retrace steps back to the start.

Weston-sub-Edge. Church and moat

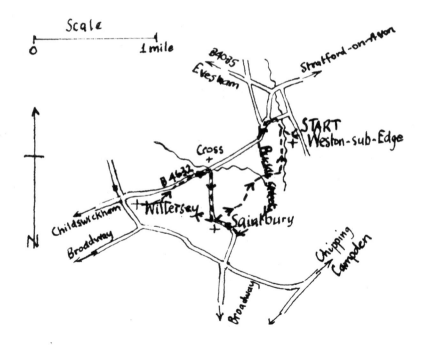

Walk 23

'The Footpath Way in Gloucestershire' — Around Weston and Willersey.

Theme: An exploration of the area of the north Cotswolds described by Algernon Gissing in his book 'The Footpath Way in Gloucestershire' (1924).

Start and finish: St. Lawrence's Church, Weston-sub-Edge.

Getting there: Weston-sub-Edge lies on the A46 (B4632), four miles NE of Broadway and 11 miles SW of Stratford-on-Avon.

Route of walk: Weston-sub-Edge — Buckle Street — Saintbury — Willersey — Saintbury Cross — Weston-sub-Edge.

Distance: Five miles.

Summary of terrain: Mostly reasonably easy walking along footpaths. The steep climb up Buckle Street can be muddy. A short stretch of unavoidable road walking along B4632.

O.S. Sheet: Landranger 150 — Worcester and the Malverns (1¼ inches to 1 mile).

Starting point grid ref: 128406.

Parking: In Weston-sub-Edge..

Refreshments: Seagrave Arms, Weston-sub-Edge. Bell Inn, Willersey.

Recommended reading: 'The Footpath Way in Gloucestershire.' Algernon Gissing, Dent. 1924.

Theme

This walk, the most northerly in the selection, starts at Weston-sub-Edge, where the Cotswolds meet with the Vale of Evesham, and climbs Roman Buckle Street (Part of Ryknild Street), to visit Saintbury church. From here it descends over fields to Willersey and then heads back to take in the remainder of Saintbury before returning over fields back to Weston.

Rolling countryside, fine views, attractive villages — no additional ingredient is required to justify the inclusion of the north Cotswolds in the selection. Yet extra appeal is provided by Algernon Gissing's book, 'The Footpath Way in Gloucestershire', which, although published as long ago as 1924 and out of print, is widely accepted as one of the most appealing of the many books written on the Cotswolds.

The author, brother of the novelist George Gissing, lived for many years at Willersey and his love and knowledge of the history and wild life of the neighbourhood are revealed in highly readable prose. He freely acknowledges his debt for much of his information to William Smith, parish clerk of Saintbury, and church bass-viol player, a roadmender for much of his life and yet a man of exceptional qualities, whose photograph can still be seen inside the church and whose grave, marked by a rugged cross, lies in the churchyard.

Weston-sub-Edge, in which parish lies the celebrated Dover's Hill of Cotswold Olympicks fame, is a village of elegant houses, several of which date from the 17th century, with scarcely a trace of lowland influence. Of particular interest is the site of the moated manor house of the Giffard family in the field behind the church. The surviving mounds indicate that the house was a substantial one and the church guide tells us that it was surrounded by orchards and fishponds, and had its own mill nearby.

Buckle Street, a section of Roman Ryknild Street extending from Bourton-on-the-Water into Yorkshire (see also Walk 20) is a delightful green lane climbing between hedges up to Saintbury church. Gissing knew it well and lamented the practice of tipping near its meeting with the road at Weston — sadly still something of a problem. His friend, the roadmender, often worked in the quarry near the top of the hill and Gissing devotes a whole chapter to the 'quarrs' such as this, describing the wild flowers found there in considerable detail.

Both Saintbury and Willersey are the subject of individual chapters in Gissing's book and it is interesting to compare the villages as we find them today with the author's descriptions of 65 years ago. Tiny Saintbury still boasts a few of the cherry trees that made its Cherry Wake famous and its modern residents maintain its old-world appearance despite all the changes wrought over the intervening years. Willersey, by contrast, has grown considerably. Church, school, inn, pond — all remain from Gissing's time, as do the spacious greens and the traditional Cotswold stone cottages, but the peaceful life of a main-road village of the 1920s is, alas, no more.

Route Directions

Leave the churchyard at the far right-hand corner and follow the footpath over the field, passing the remains of the moat on the left. Cross a stile near a power pole. Go through a kissing gate and over a bridge and then skirt a field, keeping a hedge on the right. Pass between houses and turn left and then right along a metalled road to reach the B4632 (formerly the A46). Turn left. Keep on along this road until a bridleway sign indicates straight on at a sharp right bend. This is Buckle Street, a section of Roman Ryknild Street.

Climb steadily until a fork is reached soon after a footbridge on the right. Fork right and climb through woodland, keeping to the right-hand extremity of the woods. Eventually, at the top of the slope, a track leads to a road at Saintbury. Turn right (no pavement) and descend to the church, which is approached at a footpath sign on the left by a house.

William Smith's grave is on the left side of the churchyard and is marked by a rugged cross.

After seeing the church, return to the gate and turn left to follow the footpath sign at the foot of the steps. The path crosses two fields, leaving the second by a stile about 70 yards from the bottom right-hand corner. From the stile, fork left and then turn right immediately before reaching a road. The path descends through an orchard and crosses a stile to follow a hedge on the right. Willersey church lies ahead. Cross another stile and keep straight on for the churchyard, which is entered through a kissing gate.

Leave through the main gate and walk along Church Street to the main street. The Bell Inn is on the left. After seeing the village, retrace the walk through the churchyard and as far as the first stile beyond, climbed earlier. About 30 yards beyond, cross a stile on the left and in 30 yards, cross another and go through a handgate. Keep a hedge on the right. Ignore a stile, also on the right. Cross a fence and go through a gate to reach the B4632. Turn right along it for the short walk to Saintbury Cross (no pavement).

Climb the lane up to Saintbury and, after seeing the village, follow the public footpath sign on the left a short distance up the hill from the church footpath. (Yellow arrows serve as a guide for the remainder of the walk.) After passing farm buildings, keep a fence on the left over the first field and a hedge on the right, crossing two stiles. Keep a row of trees on the left, cross a stile, and go through a gate to reach Buckle Street, climbed earlier.

Cross the lane and go over the stile opposite. Keep a hedge on the right. After the next stile, cross a plank bridge and turn left, keeping a hedge and a stream on the left. Cross two stiles and a footbridge. Turn right along the side of the next field with the stream on the right. Cross a series of stiles to reach the moated field by the church, crossed at the start of the walk.

Plaque on Sudeley Lodge, Winchcombe

Walk 24

Where kings and queens have trod — A Winchcombe area walk.

Theme: The many royal associations formed over the centuries with the Saxon borough of Winchcombe and its neighbourhood.

Start and finish: Hailes Abbey car park.

Getting there: Hailes Abbey lies a mile east of the B4632 (formerly the A46), two miles NE of Winchcombe.

Route of walk: Hailes Abbey — Beckbury Camp — Campden Lane — Lynes Barn — Deadmanbury Gate — Parks Farm — Sudeley Lodge — Sudeley Castle — Winchcombe — Cotswold Way (Puck Pit Lane) — Hailes Abbey.

Distance: 9¾ miles.

Summary of terrain: A few longish steady climbs but generally fairly easy walking along footpaths.

O.S. Sheets: Landranger 150 — Worcester and the Malverns; Landranger 163 — Cheltenham and Cirencester area (both 1¼ inches to 1 mile).

Starting point grid ref: (Sheet 150) 051301.

Parking: Hailes Abbey car park (National Trust).

Refreshments: Choice of inns and cafés in Winchcombe.

Recommended reading: Winchcombe Cavalcade, Eleanor Adlard, Burrow, 1939. A Portrait of Winchcombe, D. N. Donaldson, 1978.

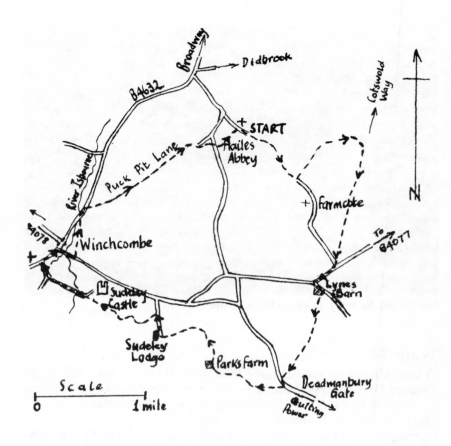

The Cotswold Way, Mark Richards, Thornhill Press, 1984.
Recommended to visit: Sudeley Castle, near Winchcombe.

Theme

Royal associations with the Cotswolds are by no means new. For
centuries, the Winchcombe area witnessed the comings of many royal
figures — Henry III, Henry VIII, Catherine of Aragon, Anne Boleyn,
Catherine Parr, George III — and for good measure this corner of the
Cotswolds can boast the legend of a murdered Saxon king and real-life
story of a lady of the manor who dressed herself to resemble Queen
Victoria!

The walk begins at Hailes Abbey, a ruin since the Dissolution of the
Monasteries in 1539. For 300 years this was a place of pilgrimage for
thousands who, like the pardoner in Chaucer's Canterbury Tales, swore
'by the blode of Crist that is in Hayles'. Like so many religious relics,

the 'Holy Blood' was later proved to be a fraud — nothing more than a concoction of honey and saffron. This in no way detracts from the former splendour of the Cistercian abbey, however, which was built by Richard, Earl of Cornwall, brother of King Henry III, in gratitude for being spared from a shipwreck on his return from a crusade. The King and Queen Eleanor were among those present at the dedication of the abbey on 5th November, 1251. Modern visitors to Hailes can tour the evocative ruins, view the extensive collection of relics in the museum and round off their visit with a glimpse of the medieval wall paintings in the nearby church, which is a century older than the abbey itself.

The stone monument known as Cromwell's Seat, below Farmcote, is one of the local mysteries. One theory is that Thomas Cromwell watched the dismantling of Hailes Abbey from here, while another maintains that the niche once held an effigy of the Virgin Mary. Beckbury Camp is older by far than any of the royal associations — dating from the Iron Age, and has never been completely excavated.

Sudeley Lodge provides the next royal association encountered on the walk. It was in 1788 that King George III visited Cheltenham and bestowed his royal approval on the growing spa. His travels brought him to Sudeley and a plaque to that effect can be seen from the footpath passing the Lodge door.

Sudeley Castle is rich in royal associations. Its origins date back to the reign of King Stephen but the older parts of the present building are largely the work of Ralph Boteler and were erected in the 15th century. Henry VIII was a frequent visitor, bringing first Catherine of Aragon and later his second wife, Anne Boleyn. A later owner was Thomas Seymour, brother of Jane, the King's third wife. He married Catherine Parr, Henry's widow, who died in childbirth in 1548 and was buried in the castle chapel. It was Emma Dent, the castle's owner during the last century, who not only bore a strong resemblance to Queen Victoria, but also posed for photographs attired in almost identical dress. She was, among other things, a collector of artistic and historic treasures, many of which can be seen by visitors today.

Winchcombe, a royal seat and possessing its own county for a time during the Saxon period, had an abbey 400 years older than that of Hailes. It was built by King Kenulf of Mercia, on whose death, according to legend, his young son Kenelm was murdered by his jealous sister Quendria. To this day, two stone coffins, one large the other small, which can be seen in the parish church, are reputed to be those of the Saxon king and his murdered son. They were found on the site of Winchcombe's abbey, of which no trace can now be seen.

Route directions

After seeing the abbey, continue up the lane leading to Farmcote. Pass a fruit farm entrance and as Farmcote appears ahead, turn left along the Cotswold Way for Beckbury Camp. Go through two gates and climb up to a beech clump. The so-called Cromwell's Seat is among the trees. The route now passes between a wall on the left and Beckbury Camp on the right. Beyond the camp, keep along the wall and then a wood before going through a gap to reach Campden Lane.

Turn right, leaving the Cotswold Way. Follow the lane until it reaches the Winchcombe road, which should be followed down to a left-hand turn signposted 'Unsuitable for motors'. Go along this lane, passing Lynes Barn Farm. Just beyond the buildings, turn right along a signposted bridleway. This climbs the edge of a field with woodland on the right, and eventually passes a derelict cottage, before keeping a wall on the left as far as a road. Turn left along the road and then right at the top of the slope, just before a layby. This is Deadmanbury Gate. In 15 yards, turn right through a gap in the hedge and keep first a wood, then a wall, on the right, as far as a road.

This road is the Salt Way. Turn left along it and in 50 yards turn right to descend a track to Parks Farm. Here, turn right under the beeches and follow the winding metalled drive to Sudeley Lodge. The bridleway passes in front of the house, with its plaque commemorating George III's visit, and then along the drive as far as a footpath opposite a cottage. Yellow arrows indicate the route along field margins. Ignore a left turn and cross a stream, aiming for the left of the castle. Beyond a kissing gate, the path forks. Take the left fork as far as the drive.

At this point, those visiting the castle should turn right and those making for Winchcombe turn left. The route crosses the River Isbourne over a bridge and climbs Vineyard Street to the B4632. Turn right for the town (the church is a short way to the left).

The route leaves Winchcombe down the steeply-sloping Castle Street. Cross the bridge and, in 50 yards, turn up a narrow alley on the left between Tan Yard Bank and Sudeley Mill Cottage. From the kissing gate at the top, keep straight on along the field path, with the river on the left, as far as a stile on the Cheltenham-Stratford road (B4632).

Turn right along the road, passing the entrance to Rushley Lane. Just before the de-restriction sign, turn right to follow the Cotswold Way along Puck Pit Lane. This eventually becomes a footpath. Watch for the yellow arrows and white dots. After crossing fields, the well-worn path passes two old oaks and turns left to meet a road. Turn right and then left along a lane by a house to a gate. Beyond, the path crosses a field to meet the abbey drive opposite the car park.

Belas Knap long barrow

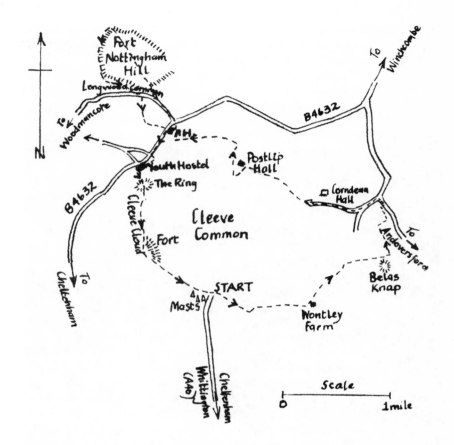

Walk 25

Cotswold Heights – Prehistoric Gloucestershire.

Theme: Prehistoric settlement on and around Cleeve Common – the highest area of the Cotswold escarpment.

Start and finish: End of approach road to masts, Cleeve Common.

Getting there: The masts on Cleeve Common (a prominent landmark) can be approached either by minor roads from Whittington, a village half-mile north of the A40 and four miles east of Cheltenham, or direct from Cheltenham, via Harp Hill and Aggs Hill (steep gradients).

Route of walk: Cleeve Common masts – Wontley Farm – Belas Knap – Corndean Lane – Postlip – Nottingham Hill – Cleeve Hill – Cleeve Cloud – the masts.

Distance: Ten miles.

114

Summary of terrain: Some steep gradients (on Cotswold standards). Care needed along edge of Cleeve Cloud on last stretch of walk. Some muddy stretches in winter.

O.S. Sheet: Landranger 163 − Cheltenham and Cirencester area (1 ¼ inches to 1 mile).

Starting point grid ref: 994248.

Parking: On approach road to masts, Cleeve Common.

Refreshments: High Roost Inn, Cleeve Hill, Golf Clubhouse, Cleeve Hill.

Recommended reading: From a Cotswold Height, J. H. Garrett, Banks, 1919 (reprinted Alan Sutton, 1988). The Cotswold Way, Mark Richards, Thornhill, 1984. Prehistoric Gloucestershire, T. Darvill, Alan Sutton, 1987. Prehistoric and Roman Sites of the Cheltenham Area, W. L. Cox, Glos. County Library, 1981.

Theme

'The top of Cleeve Hill is occupied by Cleeve Common − a great undivided stretch of greensward three miles across in one direction and two miles in another. It includes the highest ground of all the Cotswolds, some points rising to nearly 1,100 feet, whilst a large part of the area has a height of over 900 feet. These altitudes, together with the porous subsoil create a comparatively dry and bracing climate, which has brought the district a reputation for its good effect upon convalescents, and as a health resort generally.'

So wrote Dr. J. H. Garrett, Medical Officer of Health for Cheltenham and author of 'From a Cotswold Height', 70 years ago. Since then, the loss of so much wild open country, together with its flora and fauna and evidence of our prehistoric past, has given such areas as this a value beyond price. Despite the constant stream of visitors, who walk, ride, play golf, fly kites and model planes, climb rocks or merely enjoy afternoon picnics, the Common retains much of its former appeal. Sheep play a vital role in maintaining the ecological balance and the complexities of the local geology have given rise to a mixture of soils that in turn produce a richly diverse flora.

Early man has left numerous traces of occupation around the Common and the most notable of these feature on this walk. The first encountered is Belas Knap long barrow, a Neolithic burial mound dating from about 3000 BC. It measures 170 feet long by 60 feet wide (maximum) and stands 13 feet high. There were originally four chambers in which the remains of about 30 people were found when the site was excavated in the 1860s. Skilful restoration was carried out in 1931 and the horned false portal on the north side reveals superb workmanship.

The extensive fort on Nottingham Hill, a north-facing promontory 915 feet above sea level, was thought to date from the Iron Age until quite recently, when a hoard of late Bronze-age tools were discovered during ploughing. The ten-foot-high inner bank is still clearly visible, as is the outer bank beyond the intervening ditch. Altogether, about 120 acres were cut off in this way. It is believed that the Romans used this commanding site as a signal station.

Prehistoric activity on the escarpment itself has been erased to some extent by quarrying. Even so, it is well worth examining the Ring, an earthwork of Iron Age origin with traces of a hut platform visible within. The walk over Cleeve Cloud involves crossing an ancient dyke or boundary earth-work, beyond which can be seen the remains of a hill fort, also Iron Age in origin, and enclosing about two acres. This is defined by two semi-circular ramparts, each with external ditches.

Cleeve Common is protected as a Site of Special Scientific Interest (SSSI). This means that no one is allowed to interfere in any way with its unique wildlife — or for that matter, with what remains of its prehistoric relics. For that we can only be grateful.

Route directions
Go through the gate onto the Common and turn right. Keep the wall on the right to the triangulation pillar — at 1,083 feet above sea level the highest point, not only in the Cotswolds, but in the entire county. Beyond this point the gorse on the left thins out and the Common narrows. When a field wall appears on the left, follow it downhill, as far as a gate on the right opposite a Cotswold Way marker post (yellow arrow and white dot on black-and-white post). Go through the gate and follow the clear track to Wontley Farm. Turn left between the buildings and take the signposted footpath on the right indicating Belas Knap long barrow.

From Belas Knap, climb the stile near the false portal and go through a kissing gate. Keeping first a hedge, then a wall on the right, descend along the well-worn path to the road. Turn left along it. (Good view of Sudeley Castle on the right.) At a junction, turn left again along Corndean Lane. Bear right at a fork, passing Corndean Hall on the right. In about half a mile, when the footpath signposted to Cleeve Common bends to the left, keep straight on over a stile by a gate (bridleway marked by blue arrow). This path descends steeply to cross a stream by a stone footbridge. Climb the field ahead, keeping a fence on the left as far as a metal gate, after which the path follows the farm track climbing on the left. Pass through a farmyard and dip to go through a metal gate on the left (marked with a yellow arrow).

Now keep a wall on the right, go through a handgate, and then between farm buildings. This is Postlip. After passing through a metal gate, turn right, following a wall, and climb to reach the Common by a gate. At the top of the first rise, take the upper of two paths on the right. At the top turn left through another gate to follow a well-worn path. Ignore side-turns and pass through another gate to reach the open common. Eventually, after passing golf greens on the left, turn right at the club house (refreshments) — and follow the lane to meet the B4632 (Cheltenham-Winchcombe road). The High Roost Inn is 100 yards on the left.

To continue the walk, follow the lane directly opposite the lane just walked. When this lane bends to the left, keep straight on along the farm track over Nottingham Hill camp. When the track dips to a fork at two gates, take the left fork (Longwood Common on the sign-board). In 50 yards, it veers away left from the farm buildings ahead. The ramparts of the camp can now be seen on the left. Go through two metal gates and over rough ground to enter Bushcombe Wood by a stile (yellow arrow).

From the wood, go half-left up a slope. Soon the meandering path levels, widens, and descends from a gate to a road. Turn left, and in 80 yards, right, along a signposted footpath, which dips past a barn into a field. Go through a gate and keep a wall on the right in the next field. Cross a stile alongside a gate and descend another field along the same line. At the foot of the slope, instead of going through the gate ahead, turn left to cross a stile between a field gate and a hunting gate. From here, climb half-left to a gate by an oak in a wall and continue climbing to reach the road by a stile in front of the High Roost Inn.

To continue the walk, turn right along the pavement. Cross the road opposite the toilets and reach the Common once more over a stile. Bear right behind the houses, parallel to the road. Just before reaching the last building in the row — a youth hostel — turn left up the slope along a well-worn path. The Ring earthwork is soon reached. From here, climb to the right, passing to the right of a Cotswold Way black-and-white marker post, to gain the crest of the ridge.

Keep on along this fine scenic route, aiming for Cleeve Cloud rock face, visible ahead. This entails crossing several prehistoric defensive ditches and old quarry hollows. The masts can now be seen, away to the left, and the clear grassy track leads back to the start.